The Games Teacher

Activities and Resources for KS3 to PGCHE

By

Joanna Smithies

RB

Rossendale Books

Published by Lulu Enterprises Inc.
3101 Hillsborough Street
Suite 210
Raleigh, NC 27607–5436
United States of America

First published in paperback 2015
Category: Education
Copyright Joanna Smithies © 2015
ISBN : 978-1-326-48863-5

Contents

Acknowledgements...9

Chapter 1 – Introduction 10
   About this book..10
   How to use this book 11
   Game Rules...12
   Just before we start 14
   The Players...16

Chapter 2 – Starter Activities 20
   Key Word Activity...20
   Snowball/Think,Pair,Share...22
   Key Word/Key Phrase Learner Conversations................23
   Word search..24
   Floor Flow Chart...25
   Checking in...27
   Who am I?...28
   Progress organiser 29
   How old?...30
   Box mad 31
   I Already Know..33
   KWL...34
   I Know This.....35
   Thunks..36
   Roll The Dice 37
   Props 38
   Preparation Prompt..39
   Complete Me...40
   Symbol Objectives...41
   On this day... 42
   Debate Sticks 43
   Ask me about.... 45

Chapter 3 – Plenary Activities 46
   Checking out 46
   Traffic light evaluation...49
   Student turns Teacher..50
   Hot Spot 51
   Progress organiser 52
   Pair Share Reflections 53

Quick post it evaluation 54
Just A Minute 55
Elevator Pitch 56
Peer Prosecutors 57
Text Me/Tweet Me 58
Heads Up 59
Ask the Expert 60

Chapter 4 – Group Work 61
Random Group Selection Techniques 62
Round Robin Brainstorming 63
Snowball 64
Jigsaw 66
Partners 68
Trade Exhibition 69
Spectacles 71
Carousel 72
Circle View 73
Spy in the Camp 74
Silent Praise 75
Group/Pair selection Techniques 76
Playing Card Selection Techniques 78
Group Presentations 79
Random Objects 79
Question Time 80
Peer Assessment 81
As seen on TV 82

Chapter 5 – Assessment For Learning 83
Matching Games 83
Terminology Bingo 85
I am.... 86
Key Word Game (Verbosity) 87
Case Studies 88
Odd One Out 89
Play Your Cards Right 90
Teach and Listen 91
Read All About It 92
Anonymous Questions 93
Assessment Practice 94
Learner Devised Revision 95
Picture This 96
Mini Whiteboard Q & A 97

Snakes and Ladders 98

Question Jenga 99

Number Crunching 100

Sock it to me 101

Table Graffiti 102

Chapter 6 – Demonstrations 103

Work sheets 104

Questioning 105

Using learners as a resource 106

Chapter 7 – Workshops 107

Starting the session 109

Self directed learning 110

Linking theory and practice 113

Music in the classroom/workshop 115

Chapter 8 – Digital Technologies for Teaching, Learning & Assessment 116

Preparing your learners 117

Smartboards 119

Smart tools 120

Keyword Dice 120

Random Word Generator 122

Question Flippers 123

Random Group Picker 124

Timers 125

Games and Quizzes in the Smart Notebook 126

Smart Notebook and MS Office for visual target setting 128

Internet based resources 130

Wordle 130

Triptico Plus 131

Socrative 133

Nearpod 134

Google Drive 135

Virtual Learning Environment (VLE) 136

As a tool for assessment 137

VLE quizzes and games 138

Powerpoint Quizzes 139

Powerpoint for presentations 141

Prezi 142

Google Classroom 143

Digital dictionaries 145

Digital Glossaries 146

WIKI *147*

Flipped Classroom *148*

Flickr *150*

Youtube *151*

Podcasting *152*

Blogging *153*

Pinterest *154*

Trello *155*

QR Codes *157*

Augmented reality *158*

Chapter 9 – Reflection & Evaluation 160

Learning Journal *161*

Emotional Intelligence (EI) *162*

Themed EI *163*

Reflective Log *164*

Shoebox Activity *165*

Chapter 10 – The Hidden Curriculum 166

Embedding Maths *167*

Maths teasers *168*

Maths Trivia *168*

Health and Safety Quiz *169*

Embedding English *170*

Correct Me *170*

Comprehension *171*

Spell and define *172*

Glossary of terms *173*

Embedding Equality and Diversity *174*

Languages *176*

Chapter 11 – The Wow Factor 177

Picture the scene… *179*

Postcards Home *180*

Differentiation Station *181*

And finally... 182

Reading List 183

References 184

Acknowledgements

First of all thank you to all my colleagues and student teachers, past and present for your creativity and passion for teaching and learning. In particular, my colleagues Gerard Stanton, Richard Wibberley and Joanne Ivers, who are outstanding, innovative practitioners. Sarah Grisbrook, my ILT guru for her considerable contribution of authoring chapter 8. My critical friends Dr Janet Hobley and Anne Parfitt, your reviews were invaluable. The creative and talented Adam Charnock for the original illustrations and Cherie Vaughan, Nicole Astbury and Holly Davies for the book cover under the expert guidance of Joanna Spicer, Sam Henderson and Nathan Cox with permission from University Centre Stockport College. Contributions from the following and their permission to include their activities and resources in this book; Kate Whelen, Alison Williams, Marie Dodd, Sally Anne Schofield, Emma Blake, Laura Redford, Sara Mir Haydri, Janet Hobley, Ron Honey, Victoria Foxwell, Gary Taylor, Benedicta Cyril Obiagwu, Eleanor Boyce, Louise Heywood, Jackie Baddeley, Carla Salamone and Heather Stanway.

Disclaimer:

Every effort has been made to acknowledge the originators of any of the resources and activities used in this book.

Chapter 1 – Introduction

About this book

This book has been about 10 years in the writing. In that time whilst working within Teacher Education I have gathered, experienced, observed and created a multitude of ideas and resources for activities which can be adapted and evolved into many guises to be used within a range of curriculum areas. It's the concept behind the idea that makes it adaptable. So my first tip is to delve into all the areas within the book as you may find a resource or activity which you can turn, twist and change to suit your own area of specialism.

Having taught all levels over the last 21 years from entry level to degree I make suggestions here and there where you can design the activity to suit the level. You can then use these ideas to differentiate the resource if you have groups with markedly different needs and levels.

There are such a lot of good books out there for both student and experienced teachers that there was the temptation not to fill this toolkit with theory as it is so well resourced elsewhere. However, it is vital that you understand the theory behind the concept to appreciate how and why it works but I have kept it to only where it's pertinent.

 A well designed and planned activity is a dynamic tool for managing behaviour. As behaviour management is probably the most ubiquitous chore for most teachers then having a toolkit full of exciting, interesting and challenging activities will certainly support a more engaging learning environment and in turn focus students on the task in hand if it's enjoyable and challenging enough.

I hope you and your students have lots of fun learning with these activities.

How to use this book

Each activity includes an indication of which levels of learning they are suitable for although you will know your learners and how much they need to or can be challenged.

The following symbols are used throughout the toolkit:

 this symbol denotes differentiation. I have made suggestions where you can adapt the activity to differentiate. I also suggest how the activity meets the need to differentiate.

 this symbol is used where I feel a little support or some points need to be shared to help you to deliver the activity successfully.

 This symbol is used if I want to point out a word of warning.

 This symbol is used to signify the key indicators of quality teaching and learning as proposed by Ofsted.

 Is the acronym used for assessment for learning and suggests what is being assessed.

The key indicator and assessment signposts are a general suggestion. You may take account of other indicators depending on your version and theme of the activity.

Hopefully you'll have some sort of idea of whether you are planning a long or short activity, a starter or plenary, or a group work activity so you might start with that section of the book. However, if you're not inspired, look in other sections as even just a part of an activity can be transformed into a new one.

It's all about being creative and taking a risk. I promise you, you will enjoy it as much as your learners if you try something new.

Although there are activities within the book targeted to specific curriculum areas and learner levels, I do want you to consider that the majority of activities are adaptable. Just think about the learning that comes from the resource or activity and you'll find a way to make it work for your learners. I do make suggestions in the spirit of differentiation to recommend how some may be adapted to suit different levels.

Game Rules

Variety for varieties sake?

It's always a temptation to fill a lesson with as many activities as possible to keep everyone focussed and busy. You need to make time for the learners to absorb the new knowledge. You don't want to confuse them by moving too quickly onto something else. However, you might create resources and activities that build learning, so, if you are going to go to the trouble of preparing resources and activities, try to make the most of them. For example, if the students make a poster or fill in work sheets, try to use them again during the lesson to refer back to or use as a plenary or prepare a resource that you can add to as the lesson progresses.

As you'll see in the Do's and Don'ts section, although it's great to have some fun in the classroom, the activity should serve a purpose too. Remember, some of your learners may be paying a lot of money to attend your programme so it's vital that they leave in the knowledge that they have learned.

Questioning techniques

I could probably write a whole book on questioning techniques (now there's an idea!) but regardless of what activity is being played out or what resource is being used, the challenge, assessment and motivation comes from your questioning techniques. How else do you know if they are learning? I would urge you to take advantage of any development activities your institution offers to help you improve your techniques as this is something that only comes with practice and knowing the different strategies you can employ.

While learners are working on an activity you must continuously question them. This might be just to help them move forward if they are stuck, or question decisions to ensure it's not just guess work. This is also another opportunity to offer praise, the best motivator there is. Your constant presence and questioning also ensures group work doesn't descend into chit chat off topic and motivates them to continue to engage.

Creating a professional environment

Ground rules. There has to be ground rules!

You must lay down the rules at the start of the lesson and for each activity, even if you have created some in induction (which should be displayed). You need to foster an environment of respect and acceptable behaviour. Don't punish the whole class by stopping the activity just because one or two are not behaving as required. Make sure you and your department have a clear disciplinary policy so you can deal with those who don't want to learn or just spoil it for everyone else.

If you provide good quality resources, they are more likely to respect them and want to engage with them. Scraps of paper will be treated as such. Make good use of your print services, you don't have to spend hours making them yourself.

Do's and Don'ts

Do:

Make sure the activity is relevant/topical. The first 'don't' is don't do fun for funs sake. The activity must have a purpose, value and enable you to assess learning.

Use good quality resources that can be used again and shared e.g. laminate card activities – although initially time consuming and expensive will save you time and money in the long run. Scraps of paper end up being screwed up, chucked around and/or defaced.

Try to get more than one activity out of a resource. You can add to the resource to challenge further or create discussion following the activity.

Build in self assessment/reflection following any learning activity. This also gives valuable feedback for you to reflect on the effectiveness of the design.

Make sure you introduce the activity fully with clear instructions. Tell them, or even better, get them to tell you why they are doing it.

Ensure you have enough time to complete the activity and consolidate learning from it.

Differentiate – bear in mind that some may finish an activity before others so need additional tasks, throwing in a pertinent question to consider/discuss can do the trick. Have different levels of the same resource.

Don't:

Don't do fun for funs sake. Yes it's always good to let the students have some fun but do try to make it topical/relevant – *see starter activities*.

Don't use resources until you have tried them out first, particularly if you are relying on technology. Share with a colleague as they might spot something you've missed.

Don't make it too complicated. If it is quite a complicated process, work out how you can split it into several small activities, building on learning as you go.

Don't let an activity drag on too long – it gets boring for the students and behaviour may then become a problem.

Don't presume that adults don't like playing games and making posters. Yes they do if its relevant, challenging and they learn from it.

Don't give up! Figure out what didn't work and adapt it and try again – you'll get there in the end if the initial concept is appropriate and worth pursuing.

Just before we start
A little bit of theory

Remember Bloom? Benjamin Bloom (1913 – 1999) was an educational psychologist who worked on classifying educational objectives. From his research and scholarly activity, he produced what is known as Bloom's Taxonomy which is still used today within teacher training and planning for learning as an essential element for educators around the world.

When I plan lessons I think of Bloom, when I'm writing lesson objectives I think of Bloom, when I produce resources I think of Bloom, when I use questioning techniques I think of Bloom. It's such a simple but highly effective tool for you to ensure you are pitching your lesson at the right level, sequencing it correctly to ensure success and progression and also making sure you add elements of challenge.

There are a number of versions of the taxonomy around in terms of words used but the meaning and sequencing remains the same. I'm not going to spend any more time giving you a lecture on a theory you should already have studied but do want to urge you to remind yourself of the taxonomy and use it every day for one purpose or another. As a quick reminder, the sequence goes from low level learning to high as below:

Evaluation   *High level learning*

Synthesis

Analysis

Application

Understanding

Knowledge   *Low level learning*

So when you are planning and resourcing your lessons, refer to the taxonomy for your starting point and where you want to use it to differentiate resources and activities.

VAK

Another blast from the past. This acronym refers to the basic learning styles of visual, auditory and kinaesthetic . There is still and probably always will be debate about how we should plan and deliver our lessons around specific learning styles but I think we all agree that we should be aware of learning styles when planning for learning. My colleagues and I tend to refer to them as preferences rather than styles. We believe that learners have a preference rather than a style, so although they prefer to learn in a particular way, it's our responsibility to help them learn in other ways. This gives them the ability to adapt more readily to different learning situations and adds an element of challenge.

I do find it a bit simplistic to label what are individual people into a category of learning styles when they may have that style based on past instructional styles such as school experiences, lack of opportunity to experience different learning methods, peer pressure (What! You're reading a book!!) etc. Personally, I feel it is our opportunity to provide an environment that exposes our learners to a variety of learning methods and strategies so that as they progress through education work and life, they can adapt their learning style to the situation as it arises.

The Players

How young people and adults learn.

Take a little time to think about the last time you learnt something that you still remember. Why did you engage in it in the first place? What made it interesting? What reminds you of it from time to time?

Why did you engage in it in the first place? Something sparked your interest, be it relevant to an interest or hobby, your profession or out of curiosity. We presume that our learners are with us for at least one of these reasons; although there are the exceptions with some younger learners. Therefore it is vital that every lesson should make sure that they leave with something new to think about or do to make it worth the effort of engaging in it.

What made it interesting? Maybe it was the approach used that kept you engaged. Were there visuals that were interesting or different? Did the resources help you to follow the topic easier? When you are designing your activities and resources think to yourself, 'would I enjoy this? Is it interesting and challenging enough to engage my learners?' You can also appeal to their interests outside the classroom. I once observed a Functional maths lesson where the tutor copied a brochure from a mobile phone company showing all the different tariffs for different phones. The learners were tasked to find the best deal based on specific needs through a series of questions. Calculations were used and lots of debate about different methods to assess features.

For the higher level or work based learner, relate it to what they already do or may be expected to do. Case studies are great in this instance.

What reminds you of it from time to time? This is where creativity comes in. One of the best tricks I once played was to put something at the front of the classroom conspicuously covered up and it sparked great interest from the learners as they walked in. How good it was that we then had a heated discussion of what it might be instead of the sometimes chaotic start getting everyone to settle down. I then discussed the lesson objectives which helped them to guess what it was. It was actually a very old fashioned piece of equipment long since updated and by comparing the parts and usage options to the one being studied that day it made for a memorable lesson the learners talked about for weeks after. They all seemed to understand and remember that particular machine too!

The 14–15 players

So you go to work one day and suddenly find yourself timetabled for a class of 14–15 year olds. Not what you signed up for? The progression of the national curriculum to include vocational options when choosing GCSE subjects has developed partnerships with local colleges and so we find school children joining our college students. Your teacher training may not have included specific sessions on how to teach these much younger learners so some guidance on what to expect and strategies to use would be useful. There are a number of good books for you to dip into and some are listed in the reading list at the end of this book.

For most of us, this was a particularly difficult time as we evolved from being a child to an adult. Physical and social pressures and issues dominated our thoughts and actions and for some, were on the last leg to leaving education behind. However, along with the negative, there are also positive changes that we can tap into. At this age they are starting to develop reasoning skills, problem solving skills, understand consequences of actions and start to think more independently (Bostock & Wood 2012).

This can be a confusing time for these learners as their traditional learning experience of a pedagogical approach is suddenly replaced by an androgogical one. For some, this is an exciting and new experience they will embrace with enthusiasm, for others, they will be completely out of their comfort zone and not sure what is expected of them. For some, it is freedom overload and throw the usual rules out of the window. So it's important that you make sure all your young people feel comfortable, safe and understand what is expected of them.

Your challenge in terms of resources and activities, is to provide interesting and engaging sessions based on their interests and experiences. Get to know your learners, what makes them tick, make it relevant. Chunk learning, in other words, short bursts of activity and change the style (VAK) to ensure inclusive learning.

The 16–18 teen teams

Often referred to as the younger learners, they are similar in many ways to our 14–15 learners but have gained the confidence to challenge, not always in a positive way! They are more aware of their own identity and are not influenced so much by peer pressure. So here, you need to be careful in your planning, particularly with group work tasks, how these groups are put together to ensure you have cohesion. For me, I find they willingly engage more if you provide opportunities for them to challenge, they just love to share their opinions and ideas. Pose controversial or opposing questions such as 'smacking children is the best way for them to learn right from wrong'. Your classroom management skills are definitely needed here.

The grown ups

We call these our adult learners. Very much individuals but may be more habitual in their actions and learning styles so can be harder to change the way they learn. However, they bring with them life experiences which should be used within your sessions to enrich the learning environment. This is where diversity plays an important role in the learning environment. Use their experiences and prior knowledge and understanding to celebrate and challenge. In group work for instance, you can create differentiated groups to allow for peer teaching which challenges the stronger learners and brings a variety of ages, abilities and experiences together.

Adults have the ability to engage in meaningful reflection and some element of reflection or evaluation of learning is usually standard practice in learning levels of 3 and above. I feel it is vital that learning is reflected upon and evaluated where appropriate during a session and always at the end of a session – *see Reflection for strategies to promote.*

The Winners

These are the learners that turn up, engage and strive to reach their potential. You play a big part in making this happen by providing effective, enjoyable and challenging sessions. Olympian, Jessica Ennis promotes the 6 keys to success in sport as:
1. Mental toughness
2. Hunger to achieve
3. People skills
4. Sports and life knowledge
5. Breaking barriers
6. Planning for success
(*livingforsport.skysports.com*)

Translated into education, this means you should aim to
1. Challenge
2. Take advantage of using success stories and guest speakers from industry
3. Use collaborative learning techniques improving communication skills
4. Consider promoting emotional intelligence
5. Promote a 'can do' attitude and plan for differentiation
6. Ensure every learner achieves something in each and every lesson

The Losers

Who's fault is it, yours or theirs? Probably a bit of both. However, if you make it an enjoyable and challenging experience and embed the key skills to success, at least you know you've done your very best to make a difference and turn a loser into a winner. We can't 'fix' everyone, but if we can for just one, then it's all worthwhile.

Game on...

Chapter 2 – Starter Activities

A good starter activity sets the pace and tone of the session. It can help in so many ways:

- Focusses students attention straight away
- A great way to introduce the topic
- Can be revisited as a consolidation/plenary activity at the end of the session
- A handy initial assessment tool to test prior learning and understanding

Certainly if you have very chatty groups who are hard to settle down, having a simple activity ready on the tables as they walk in is a very effective way to get them focussed quickly. It also gives early arrivers something to do.

You'll notice that the majority of the starter activities don't require much input from you! The best resource you have is your learners so use them. For new or nervous teachers this is the best strategy as it takes the heat off you while you settle into the lesson.

Some starter activities can also be used as plenaries or consolidation of learning at a specific point in the lesson to refocus. You decide the relevant point to introduce the activity.

Key Word Activity – *all learning levels*

An easy to prepare and fun key word game is to spell out a word vertically and task the students to write a word using each letter relevant to the word or topic – as in the example following:

H   hibernate

A   access point

R   raw file

D   digital data

D   debugger

R   remote access

I   IMAP

V   virtual memory

E   encryption

Just print off one page for each student and instruct them not to copy. To take the game further, you can have a competition at the end. Each one in turn offers their answer to a particular letter to ensure you engage all students and they can only score a point if they have written something no one else has. A little prize at the end adds to the competition.

 each learner is involved in this activity as the task initially requires independent thinking. Your usually quiet learners have the opportunity to shine

 make sure you have pre prepared at least one answer for each of the letters in case all learners are struggling with one of the letters . Maybe add a relevant picture as well for your visual learners – using a picture as a background watermark always looks good

 prior knowledge and understanding, independence, English, assessment

prior knowledge and understanding, English

Snowball/Think,Pair,Share – *all learning levels*

You'll need some different coloured post its for this. Each learner is given a post it and asked to compose a definition of a word. Then put into pairs, issue a different coloured post it, and ask the pairs to compare answers and turn into one answer and write on the new post it. Then create a group of four, each pair compares their answers and on another coloured post it come up with a new group answer. These are in turn fed back to the whole group – you can pick out key words to write on the board or flip chart (an opportunity to give praise). This can then be compared to your prepared definition.

each learner is involved in this activity as the first task requires independent thinking then peer support and teaching naturally occurs as the activity progresses to the next stage

independence, English, assessment, independence, stretch and challenge, group work, feedback

prior knowledge and understanding, self, peer, communication, reflection and evaluation

Key Word/Key Phrase Learner Conversations – *high level learning, possibly mid level learning – see* *below*

Display a word, phrase or even better, a contentious statement on the board. Students work in pairs sitting opposite each other to discuss. To ensure one doesn't dominate the activity, give each one a specific time to talk while the other just listens then swap over.

This activity can be adapted in lots of different ways depending on what you are assessing. It could be a new topic just to see what they already know. Peer teaching happens naturally if you use this activity. You can task them to talk about how they use xxx in the workplace.

You can turn it into a debate if using a contentious statement e.g. 'smacking a pre school child teaches them right from wrong at an early age'.

 – if your session requires critical thinking skills, this starter will help to get them in the zone

 I've classed this as higher level learning only because I'm a bit wary of how the younger/lower level learner will engage – it's such a temptation to have a chat off topic. You will know your learners enough to gauge whether they will cooperate in this type of activity

stretch and challenge, assessment, pace, group work, prior knowledge and understanding

prior knowledge and understanding, peer, communication, reflection and evaluation

Word search – *low level learning*

Now I'm not a lover of word search and always challenge my trainee teachers on their choice of this activity. Usually it's used as an easy option as there are a number of good websites that will create them for you. It's also used as an extension activity, a handy resource to pull out when needed. My objections are that it doesn't measure learning, is not much of a challenge and personally I find them boring. So let's make this more interesting and also build in differentiation.

You can create 3 levels of word search:

Level 1 – After each word is found and marked, the learner then has to write a definition of the word (or if chosen to list tools or materials used, explain what it is used for).

Level 2 – when the word is found, put it into a sentence.

Level 3 – write a paragraph using all the words once found.

 – I hope you've already recognised that the levels go from easy to hard so you can give the learners the level you feel will challenge them the most

 differentiation, stretch and challenge, English, independence

 self, English

Floor Flow Chart – *all levels*

I observed one of my trainee teachers using a flow chart on the floor for small groups to create and it gave me lots of ideas to expand on the original concept (*thanks Emma*).

In many areas, learners have to learn sequences which can be displayed pictorially using a flow chart approach. You will need room to do this so is probably more suitable in a workshop environment unless you are lucky to have a big classroom or could choose to put on the wall. In the workshop, it would be more competitive if each group can't see the others.

It doesn't really matter at what point the learning is, they may know nothing or a little bit of the particular topic but you need to be sure they have just enough knowledge to make some considered decisions.

You will need each step on A4 and laminated (you can add some arrows too). With no initial introduction on the topic or clues to give them, ask them to create the sequence on the floor as best they can at this stage. The lesson then proceeds and you can either stop at planned points for them to reconsider their chart or wait to the end to re consider and put in the correct sequence. You can create a sense of competition by saying how many they have right at each stage but without pointing out which ones.

There are lots of positives to this activity and if you refer to the Do's section, you will see you've ticked a lot of boxes.

 – If you are stopping to re consider the flow chart in stages, direct one of the weaker learners to make the changes when you are sure they know what changes to make (this makes learning 'stick'). Mix up the groups with strong and weak learners together to promote peer support but do be observant to ensure the stronger learners don't take over and do all the work – maybe allocate 'roles' for the activity (see group work).

if you only have a small group use the interactive whiteboard. Prepare the pieces of the flow chart scattered across the board and invite each learner in turn to put one in place. Too many learners to do this? Then ask the stronger learners to do the first attempt (challenging) then the weaker ones complete it at the end (easier but confirming learning and adds a sense of achievement). Alternatively, create a washing line from string, prepare the cards and enough pegs.

 stretch and challenge, assessment, structure, group work, differentiation, prior knowledge and understanding

prior knowledge and understanding, peer, communication, linking theory to practice, reflection and evaluation

Checking in – *all levels*

If you are teaching work based learning groups the check in can be asking them to give an example of how they have used learning from the programme in the work place. (see also Plenaries, Checking Out). This will provide a focus and maybe enable you to link prior learning and experience to what is to come next.

all learners have the opportunity to engage from the start of the session

Q & A, feedback, assessment, differentiation, prior knowledge and understanding, equality and diversity

prior knowledge and understanding, self, employability, linking theory to practice, reflection and evaluation

Now at the risk of contradicting myself with the warning not to do fun for fun's sake, this next suggestion is really for those groups who are really hard to settle down, get focused and who love to talk. I challenge you to get creative in that if they like to do something that threatens to disrupt learning then think of a way of using it to your advantage.

Settling in

Monday mornings means that learners just have to tell their friends what they did at the weekend. So why not start by structuring these conversations. Space allowing, get them to stand up in a circle – easier to manage this way – and each has to share one thing they did at the weekend. You may have to lay down some ground rules beforehand to ensure the contribution is suitable but at the least it gets their 'news' off their chests (make sure you join in too but keep it impersonal).

Using mobile phones is always a frustration for teachers. You can at this point ask them to hold up their phones then ask them all to switch them off while you are watching.

Organisations have their own rules about using mobiles and I expect you also have a ground rule that covers them too but in my opinion they just don't belong in the classroom unless you have planned an activity where they are allowed to be used, as a calculator, dictionary or camera for instance. However, you can use them as a bargaining tool – see **Re-energising**.

Who am I? – *all levels*

This is another starter that can also be used as a plenary. You need to make cards with key words on them, at least enough for all members of the class. Keep the cards in a bag or hat and each learner takes a card in turn and has to describe what the word is without saying the word. The person who gets it right goes next.

 – make sure you have enough time for all learners to take a turn. You may want to choose what words to give them to make sure all are appropriately challenged.

 use a timer to make sure there is enough time for everyone to take their turn

 Q & A, stretch and challenge, assessment, differentiation, prior knowledge and understanding

 prior knowledge and understanding, peer, communication, English

Progress organiser – *all levels*

See **Plenary activities**

Maths Challenge

In order to embed core and functional skills, you can take advantage of starter activities to include maths which might not otherwise be a part of your curriculum.

There are lots of fun maths challenges available on the web and you should make every effort to contextualise the challenge to make it more meaningful.

Here are some quick basic challenges:

Using the numbers 1 7 7 7 7, make the answer 100.

They will try all sorts of calculations, the most frequent answer given being 99 (7x7 +7x7 +1)

The answer is 177 – 77 = 100

 stronger learners can be chosen to show the correct calculation on the board

stretch and challenge, assessment, maths

maths

How old? – *all levels*

Mark asked his grandma how old she was. Rather than giving him a straight answer, she replied:

"I have 6 children, and there are 4 years between each one and the next. I had my first child, your Uncle Peter when I was 19. Now the youngest one, your Auntie Jane) is 19 herself. That's all I'm telling you!"

How old is Marks grandma?

(if I have to give you the answer – back to school you should go!)

stretch and challenge, assessment, maths

maths

Box mad – *all levels*

I have ten boxes which I want to pack into crates. Each crate can carry a maximum of 25 kg.

But I only have three crates, and the total weight of the boxes is 75kg:

15 kg, 13kg, 11 kg, 10 kg, 9 kg, 8 kg, 4 kg, 2 kg, 2kg, 1 kg.

How can I pack the boxes into the crates?

Answer: Lots of variables available as follows -

Crate 1, Crate 2, Crate 3

{15,10}, {13,8,4}, {11,9,2,2,1}

{15,10}, {13,11,1}, {9,8,4,2,2}

{15,10}, {11,8,4,2}, {13,9,2,1}

{15,10}, {11,9,4,1}, {13,8,2,2}

{11,10,4}, {15,8,2}, {13,9,2,1}

{11,10,4}, {15,9,1}, {13,8,2,2}

{13,8,4}, {15,9,1}, {11,10,2,2}

{13,10,2}, {15,8,2}, {11,9,4,1}

{13,10,2}, {15,9,1}, {11,8,4,2}

{13,11,1}, {15,8,2}, {10,9,4,2}

(*Maths is Fun – online*)

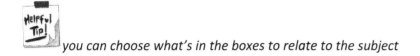 *you can choose what's in the boxes to relate to the subject*

for the stronger learners and as an extension activity, some learners are asked to calculate more than one variable

stretch and challenge, assessment, maths

maths

I Already Know – *all levels*

At the beginning of a new topic, learners write down everything they already know. This serves as an initial assessment and ensures that you don't start to teach them something they already know and gives you a dynamic start to the activity by being able to extend the knowledge into learning through questioning.

 this enables you to record every learners starting point ad plan appropriately

 feedback, assessment, structure, target setting, equality and diversity, prior knowledge and understanding

self, prior knowledge and understanding, reflection and evaluation

This activity can be extended further and used as a plenary as well with the following activities.

KWL – *all levels*

Prepare a template as a 3 columned grid as below:

What I know		
What I want to know		
What I have learnt		

Make sure you include the topic or unit title above the grid. Learners fill in the first two rows and the last one can be used as the plenary or you can bring out the grid at points throughout the session for learners to add to as learning occurs.

this enables learners to self assess and set their own targets

feedback, assessment, structure, target setting, equality and diversity, prior knowledge and understanding

self, prior knowledge and understanding, reflection and evaluation

I Know This... – *all levels*

Another version of what they already know, put learners in pairs and for a short time – 1–2 minutes, tell each other what they already know about the topic.

This can also be used as a plenary for a slightly longer length of time.

 every learner has the opportunity to engage .Hearing something for a second time and 'talking learning', helps learning stick

 be wary of who you do this with. You need to ensure you have groups you can trust not to chat off topic

 prior knowledge and understanding, feedback, stretch and challenge, assessment, group work, differentiation, independence

prior knowledge and understanding, self, peer, communication, reflection and evaluation

Thunks – *all levels*

This is another activity that is used to promote critical thinking skills so is great for higher level learners. Also, for other levels, it gets everyone focussed on the same thing and makes it easier to settle everyone down. Thunks are dilemmas or food for thought. For example:

'If my car breaks down at the side of the road, is it parked?' Or:

'If I go into a newsagents, take a magazine off the shelf, read it from cover to cover, put it back, then leave the shop, is it stealing?' (*Gilbert 2007*)

You decide the best way to deliver this – as a whole class debate, small group discussion etc. You could also take a yes/no vote before discussion then again after to see if people's minds have been changed. Do try to find a thunk linked to your subject but if you can't, here is my theory why it's a good enough reason to do it. If you can introduce something memorable, then whatever else was experienced at the same time becomes memorable. Some of my learners have said they remembered a particular class because 'that was the one when we did the thunk'. That's good enough for me.

 all learners have the opportunity to share their thoughts and opinions

 I usually have this displayed on the white board as learners enter and encourage engagement immediately. Try to make it visually appealing too by adding pictures/graphics.

 stretch and challenge, differentiation, independence

peer, communication, critical thinking

Roll The Dice – *all levels*

Depending on the size of the group, make one or more dice from thick paper or card. You can populate each side of the dice in a variety of ways:

- Questions as a recap from previous learning
- Key words for the roller to think of a question to ask someone else related to the word
- Key words that they have to talk about for 30 seconds
- Each side has a number which is related to questions you have prepared (this is a good option as you can use the dice over and over again)
- A picture clue related to prior learning or what is going to be learned

 you can make different levels of dice and group the learners appropriately

 You are probably already thinking about how you can use this for plenaries too – fabulous. You should be able to find some good templates on the web to help you make them such as this:

 don't use flimsy paper as its harder to make and can collapse

Q & A, feedback, stretch and challenge, prior knowledge and understanding, assessment, pace, structure, group work, differentiation, independence

prior knowledge and understanding, self, peer, communication, English

Props – *All levels*

Use props to intrigue learners as they settle in. They can be a clue to what the lesson is about and will focus them straight away. For example, in construction, you could have a set of tools spread out, they have to name them, give an example of what they are used for and, as a collection, guess what procedure/task they would all be used for. For added interest, if you have some old fashioned or obsolete versions, consider showing these too.

 take advantage of those learners working in the industry and the stronger ones by using their skills and experiences if they struggle with some questions e.g. Dave, what was Carl working on when you helped him find this tool?

Q & A, stretch and challenge, feedback, assessment, structure, differentiation, equality and diversity, prior knowledge and understanding

prior knowledge and understanding, self, peer, employability, English (using technical language), linking theory to practice

Preparation Prompt – *all levels*

To enthuse and give confidence when starting a new topic, share and describe the objectives/outcomes and basic content/criteria and ask one or more of the following:

What skills do you already have that you can bring to the lesson today?

What do you already know about this subject that will help you today?

When have you learnt something like this before?

This can also give you the opportunity to praise learners right from the start by confirming how skilled they are already or how their knowledge is going to be so useful for them and their peers.

 your quieter learners get the chance to shine by sharing a skill or knowledge

 it might be useful to have a list of the skills and knowledge you know they already have to use as prompts

 prior knowledge and understanding, Q & A, feedback, target setting, differentiation, equality and diversity

 prior knowledge and understanding, self, employability, communication, linking theory to practice, reflection and evaluation

Complete Me – *all levels*

Create a paragraph or page depending on level of a summary of previous learning but leave out words or ends of sentences which the learners have to insert. Have this ready on the tables for learners to start as soon as they arrive. This will get them settled and focussed quickly.

 prepare different levels related to the different abilities of your learners but always make sure there is an element of challenge.

prior knowledge and understanding, stretch and challenge, assessment, structure, English, differentiation, independence

prior knowledge and understanding, self, communication

Symbol Objectives – *low to middle levels*

Why not present your objectives as symbols and the learners have to guess what they are. This can then be a discussion point about what is going to happen in the lesson. It's fun and gets them focussed straight away. An example of this could be:

I'll let you work that one out!

 Q & A, stretch and challenge, English

 communication, English

On this day... *– all levels*

A great starter to embed diversity is to present something that is topical although not necessarily related to the lesson, or has some link to the topic to be learned.

On the week leading up to remembrance day my colleague presented pictures of images that depicted historical sights or countries emblems. He asked the learners to find the link. Once it was found or not found in some cases he revealed the link which was a poppy. The images all represented the countries who had engaged in war and lost lives. It made for a poignant and interesting discussion. A lot of younger learners tend to think World War 2 was all about Great Britain and Germany, not realising that so many others were caught up in it and other wars.

Alternatively, if a notable event happened linked to the topic, then this could be used. For example, if teaching childcare, it could be a change in the law related to children, for example, the raising of the school leaving age; age entitled to vote/marry. You could have it as a question to discuss before revealing the answer.

         Q & A, feedback, stretch and challenge, English, equality and diversity, prior knowledge and understanding

prior knowledge and understanding, self, communication, English, reflection and evaluation

Debate Sticks – *all levels*

A great starter activity that engages everyone in a debate to wake them up and get them talking. You will need to collect or buy lolly sticks and stick on them debate topics. Allow learners to take turns when you use this to pick a stick and start the debate. Some examples could be:

❖ The internet does more harm than good

❖ Swearing at work is acceptable in some cases

❖ It's wrong to judge people by the clothes they wear

❖ What is the point of human rights?

Think about the level of learner when composing your debate topics. Higher level learners can be given topics which have a variety of viewpoints, lower level learners can be given more straight forward concepts. Chair the debate rather than join in and invite the quieter ones to engage.

you could make all the topics subject relevant but its good to include some as above that develop their social and employability skills

if you have a large group where a debate could be chaotic with too many shouting out, you could put the learners in groups to discuss rather than debate

Q & A, prior knowledge and understanding, feedback, stretch and challenge, structure, group work, English, differentiation, equality and diversity, independence

 prior knowledge and understanding, self, peer, employability, communication, English, linking theory to practice, reflection and evaluation

Ask me about.... – *all levels*

This is a great recap activity to start a session but can also be used as a plenary or revision exercise.

Prepare cards that start with 'ask me about' then add the topic, for example:

- ❖ Ask me about changing a tyre

- ❖ Ask me about looked after children

- ❖ Ask me about hanging a door

Put learners in pairs with a batch of cards face down and each take a turn to select a card and read it out. Their partner then asks them questions and once they feel they have explored it enough, they swap roles.

 Every learner is engaged and peer support and learning naturally occurs. For lower level learners you may have to supplement this with written questions for them to ask.

if you only have a small group, deliver as a whole group activity but each person has to ask a question for each round of 'ask me about...'

Q & A, feedback, prior knowledge and understanding, stretch and challenge, assessment, structure, group work, independence

prior knowledge and understanding, self, peer, communication, linking theory to practice, reflection and evaluation

Chapter 3 – Plenary Activities

There is nothing worse than a hurried end to a lesson. Have you ever said 'Oh is that the time? Better clear up now and see you tomorrow'. Aim to finish ALL your lessons with some type of self or peer assessment, reflection or evaluation activity. Cowley (2006) calls this 'evaluative thinking'. She considers that:

> 'Being able to look critically at our own work, and that of others, is a
> hugely important part of the learning process. By examining what we are
> already capable of producing, we undertake the vital process of self
> evaluation' (page 135)

Cowley uses this strategy as a behaviour management tool. You want your learners to leave on a positive note and most of all to take some responsibility for what they have learned and what they can do with it. Telling themselves or someone else is a lot more powerful than you telling them.

Checking out – *all levels*

This is a particularly effective activity for learners who are work based or complete placements as part of their programme.

At the end of the lesson, they each share how they can use the learning in the workplace. Do make sure you allow some think time before you start.

You can also use checking out as an evaluation of the lesson, particularly if you have tried out a new activity. You can ask them what they enjoyed most about the lesson and challenge further by asking 'why' too. What better way to end a lesson than your learners sharing what they enjoyed.

Here is a list of handy questions you can use to ensure you don't do the same ones every time:

- ❖ How can you use this learning in the workplace?

- ❖ What have you learned today that you didn't know before?

- ❖ What was the most interesting thing you learned today?

- ❖ What was the most important thing you learned today?

- ❖ What would you like to know more about?

- ❖ What did you enjoy most in today's lesson?

- ❖ Which activity did you enjoy most and why?

- ❖ State 3 things you have learnt today

- ❖ What can you do now that you couldn't do at the start of the session?

- ❖ Why do you need to know this? (a good starter question too)

- ❖ If someone asks you 'what did you learn today?', what will you say?

- ❖ What skills have you used today?

- ❖ Which existing skills/knowledge did you use in today's lesson and how did this help?

- ❖ What do you think you did well today?

You'll notice that these are all positive affirmations. This is deliberate to make sure the lesson ends on a positive note. You'll know what they didn't enjoy by their reactions to activities and what they are struggling with when you question them throughout the lesson.

Rather than ask them all the same question, have this list handy and ask them all a different one. If you don't have much time, just choose one question, give them all 10 seconds to think of a response which has to be just one word. They then state their word in quick succession. Tell them it doesn't matter if they say the same as someone else. The important point here is that they have confirmed they have learnt something.

Contextualise the question occasionally such as 'Which tool did you find most tricky/easy to use today?'

each learner has the opportunity to share what is important to them, every learner is given a voice. You can ask questions relevant to levels of ability and understanding

Q & A, feedback, prior knowledge and understanding, assessment, target setting, differentiation, independence, equality and diversity

prior knowledge and understanding, self, employability, communication, linking theory to practice, reflection and evaluation

Traffic light evaluation – *low level*

Create a grid listing all the skills/knowledge to be learnt that day or even on a particular unit/topic. Use the traffic light system to indicate:

Green – I'm happy I know/can do this

Amber – I Know/can do some of this

Red – I don't know/can't do this

Use stickers for the colours and the learners can put them on and hand them back for you to reflect on your lesson(s) and plan future ones. An example is given below

OCR Entry level Certificate in Child Development			
Topic Physical Development Newborn Baby	Green I'm happy I know/can do this	Amber I Know/can do some of this	Red I don't know/can't do this
The characteristics of a newborn baby		●	
The needs of the newborn baby	●		
Identify the specific needs of the pre–term (premature) baby			●

 each learner self assesses and can contribute to individual target setting

prior knowledge and understanding, feedback, assessment, target setting, structure, differentiation, independence

prior knowledge and understanding, self, reflection and evaluation

Student turns Teacher – *all levels*

Instead of you firing plenary questions at your learners, ask them to come up with a question which they will ask to another learner based on that lesson or topic covered so far.

 You may want to put them in small groups to support each other in which case the group will create more than one question to put to other groups. This facilitates peer support but do be careful to have a strategy to ensure everyone has a turn asking and answering.

 you may want to use a *random name generator tool to pick out whose asking and answering to make sure people aren't 'picked on'

 Q & A, feedback, stretch and challenge, assessment, structure, group work, differentiation

 self, peer, communication, linking theory to practice, reflection and evaluation

Hot Spot – *all levels*

Divide learners into two groups. The groups create a list of questions related to the topic or unit studied.

Put a chair in the middle which is the hot spot. A member of group 1 will take the hot spot and group 2 will ask a question. If they get it right, another member of group 1 takes the hotspot and this repeats until they get a question wrong. The hot spot is then taken over by group 2.

 Make sure everyone takes a turn on the hot spot and posing a question. Keep a score to make it more competitive – do this visually on the white board or flip chart.

 You could add a phone a friend option but keep this to a minimum as one group could dominate the hot spot. To make it more fun, get them to act it out by miming the phone a friend. You could also task them to have different 'levels' of questions which carry different amounts of points to ensure everyone gets a fair chance to answer correctly.

 Q & A, feedback, prior knowledge and understanding, stretch and challenge, assessment, pace, structure, group work, differentiation, equality and diversity

 prior knowledge and understanding, self, peer, communication, linking theory to practice, reflection and evaluation

Progress organiser – all levels

A reflective learner is an effective learner. By empowering your learners with this type of activity, they will take ownership of their learning and by setting their own targets, are more likely to keep them thereby motivating them to improve.

This activity can be used for whole programmes, units or topics or even single lessons. It can be a booklet in its own right or part of a reflective journal or professional development plan. It is then a useful aid to be discussed in tutorials/progress reports.

Below is an example that you can adapt to suit your learners and programmes. The first three questions should be completed as the starter activity:

Unit 2: Construction and the Environment	
LO1: Know the important features of the natural environment that need to be protected	
What I already know	
What I want to know	
How I will learn this	
What I have learnt	
What I need to practice	

each learner has the opportunity to self assess and set their own goals

prior knowledge and understanding, feedback, assessment, structure, tsrget setting, differentiation, equality and diversity, independence

prior knowledge and understanding, self, reflection and evaluation

Pair Share Reflections – *all levels*

In pairs, each learner is given time to share with their partner one or a combination of these:

3 things I have learnt today

What I found easy today

What I found difficult today

What I can do in the future based on what I learnt today

It's important that you instruct them that this is not a conversation or they may stray off the topic. While one speaks, the other just listens.

the activity ensures everyone has the opportunity to engage. You may want to choose questions appropriate to the level of the group

make sure you time the activity so everyone has equal amounts of time to share.

feedback, assessment, structure, target setting, differentiation, equality and diversity, independence

self, communication, linking theory to practice, reflection and evaluation

Quick post it evaluation – *all levels*

If you don't have a lot of time at the end but need to be able to evaluate learning or a new activity, this could be the answer.

Give each learner a post it to write on and leave on the door on their way out. You decide what you want to know.

 this anonymous evaluation gives the weaker/quieter ones a voice

 Try to make it a positive question. You may want to know what they didn't like though so use a positive question as well to counteract it, for example 'What did you enjoy least' followed by 'What did you enjoy most?'.

 feedback, assessment, differentiation

 self, communication, reflection and evaluation

Just A Minute – *middle to higher levels*

You may have listened to the game *Just a Minute* or more recently watched it on TV. A contestant (learner) is given a word/phrase/topic to talk about for one minute. If they hesitate, the task is carried on by the person who shouts 'hesitation' and carries on for the remainder of the time. The last person talking when the minute is up gets the point.

You will have the list to decide what the person has to talk about so you can ensure everyone gets a fair chance to win. You could put learners in groups if it's impossible for everyone to have a go so the 'group' wins at the end.

Why not have prizes instead of points, this makes it so much more competitive. If choosing the group option above, do have consolation prizes too for the losing group – everyone's a winner! Use a visible electronic timer tool to add to the challenge (see **Digital technologies***).*

Despite me advising not to make starters and plenaries too lengthy, this can take quite a while so you might want to use it when you have a good 15–20 minutes to fill at the end of your planned lesson.

feedback, stretch and challenge, prior knowledge and understanding, assessment, pace, structure, group work, differentiation

prior knowledge and understanding, self, peer, communication, maths, English, linking theory to practice

Elevator Pitch – *all levels*

As an alternative to *Just A Minute* and to include lower levels, try this:

Set the scene and to make it more fun, put learners in groups spread around the classroom. Have sets of cards with floor numbers on them ranging from about 5 to 20 – you decide, and another set with a topic or key word. Then set them face down. Learners take turns selecting a topic card, another selects the floor card and has the responsibility for counting down the floors from their number down to the ground.

The learner with the topic has to talk about/ pitch their topic to the others in the elevator until it reaches the ground. All learners need to take a turn with a topic and floor card. Depending on the time you have, assemble groups accordingly, the less in the group, the quicker the activity.

 All learners get the chance to take part. You could be selective when giving out the topics to engage and challenge individual learners.

 If time is limited, you could just choose names at random and learners pitch to the whole group. You need to decide how long it takes to pass each floor. The floor counter, for example could announce each floor at 3 second intervals.

 feedback, stretch and challenge, assessment, prior knowledge and understanding, pace, structure, group work, English, maths, equality and diversity

prior knowledge and understanding, self, peer, communication, maths, English, reflection and evaluation

Peer Prosecutors – *middle to higher levels*

Following a collaborative group activity, put your learners into pairs. Inform them they are all prosecutors and need to prepare a list of evidence they are going to put to their partner following their conviction for being an outstanding member of the group during the lessons activities.

It's always good for the teacher to tell someone how good they have been but it is equally, if not more welcome, when it comes from a peer.

 everyone has the opportunity to give and receive feedback and the less confident learners will leave on a high

WARNING

you need to be sure your group is one who will cooperate with positive comments

feedback, assessment, group work, English, differentiation, equality and diversity

AFL

self, peer, communication, English, reflection and evaluation

Text Me/Tweet Me – *all levels*

I saw one of my student teachers do the *Text Me* and thought it was great, the learners really enjoyed it. Make life size copies of mobile phones showing the messages page and ask the learners to write a text to their friend telling them what they learned today. They then pass their message on for the other to read.

For *Twitter Me*, the same strategy but with a twitter page and be sure to limit them to the standard 140 characters, so this may be more suitable for higher level learners. Ask them to hand them in at the end so you can evaluate learning.

Each learner has the opportunity to engage. You may want to give them the choice of whether they want to text or tweet.

feedback, prior knowledge and understanding, assessment, English, maths, differentiation, independence – prior knowledge and understanding , self, communication, English, maths

prior knowledge and understanding, self, communication, English, maths, reflection and evaluation

Heads Up – *all levels*

There is a great mobile app for this game but very easy to make your own.

Learners are put into pairs and each in turn holds a card up to their forehead faced towards their partner. The partner has to describe what is on the card without saying the word and the card holder has to guess what's on it. Once it's guessed, the roles are reversed.

This can descend into much hilarity as it can be frustrating but in a good way. What better way to end the lesson than with a laugh. Of course this can also be used as a starter activity for recap from previous learning.

 everyone has the opportunity to engage and you could differentiate by selecting who gets which set of cards related to their level

If you don't have time to make cards then use post it notes. Cards are a better option though as they can be used time and again and for other activities such as matching words to definitions. Use a timer tool to add pace and structure.

Q & A, feedback, stretch and challenge, prior knowledge and understanding, assessment, pace, structure, group work, English, digital technology

prior knowledge and understanding, self, peer, communication, English, linking theory to practice

Ask the Expert – *all levels*

When facilitating group work activities, it often happens that learners take the opportunity to ask lots of questions about your experience and skills that are not specific to the task in hand. It's tempting to be flattered and also feel that you should reward their enthusiasm with a response. However this invariably descends into lengthy discussions off topic and distracts others from the task in hand.

If this happens a lot then why not build in an 'ask the expert' activity somewhere in the session or better still, at the end. You can instruct learners that they can ask one question each and you will sit at the front on the 'hot spot'.

everyone has the opportunity to engage

You will need to time this very carefully so it doesn't take over the session. Use a timer tool to add pace and structure.

Q & A, feedback, prior knowledge and understanding, assessment, pace, structure, group work

prior knowledge and understanding, self, peer, communication, linking theory to practice

Chapter 4 – Group Work

We all do group work activities and the learners get so used to doing them that they can become a bit of same old same old. As always, you need to think about the learning that needs to come from the activity so it is challenging and if you have big groups, you need to be sure everyone engages. Group work doesn't mean it's an opportunity for you to have a break and check your emails!

Many of the starter and plenary activities are group work activities so when reading through them, remember you can use the concept behind the activity to relate it to a new activity.

Here are my top tips for group work:

Allocate different tasks to different groups – this could be based around levels of questions being asked –

shallow   deep   profound learning

(*West–Burnham & Coates 2005*)

 Allocate groups to facilitate a peer teaching/supporting approach

 Allocate 'roles' to group members e.g.

Scribe, Chair, Presenter, Book researcher, Web researcher.

 When facilitating group work, have a list of challenging questions to 'throw in' at appropriate points.

 When facilitating group work, speak to each group as you circulate – ask challenging or enquiring questions; praise those working well together.

Use traffic light cups to help you facilitate more effectively (See **Workshops**).

To minimise the temptation to talk off topic while you are facilitating another group, make the tasks challenging/competitive by adding time constraints and competition prizes.

Random Group Selection Techniques

More often than not its good practice to select groups taking into account differentiation to ensure all learners have the same opportunity to learn and contribute. Sometimes, though, you might want to just use a random selection. Random name generators are a great way and you can prepare these on your interactive whiteboard or software readily available on the web. I have also suggested below some quick and fun ways to randomly select groups:

❖ Month of birth

❖ Length of hair

❖ Shoe size

❖ Number of siblings

❖ Height

❖ Number of colours one is wearing

❖ Furthest travelled in the world (you might need to take a map in with you)

Round Robin Brainstorming – *medium to high levels*

Class is divided into small groups (4 to 6) with one person appointed as the recorder.

A question is posed with many answers and students are given time to think about answers.

After the "think time," members of the team share responses with one another round robin style.

The person next to the recorder starts and each person in the group in order gives an answer (including the recorder) until time is called.

The recorder writes down the answers of the group members.

(*Cooperative Learning* online)

 Every learner is given the opportunity to contribute and the stronger learners can be given the role of recorder . You might want to select seating positions so that weaker learners have the opportunity to start and stronger learners challenged more to think of an original contribution.

As a behaviour management tool, give the role of recorder to a learner who otherwise is usually disruptive – this keeps them busy and out of trouble. The responsibility could even have a positive effect on them.

Q & A, prior knowledge and understanding, feedback, stretch and challenge, assessment, structure, group work, English, differentiation, equality and diversity, independence

prior knowledge and understanding, self, peer, communication, English, reflection and evaluation

Snowball – *all levels*

Also known as think–pair–share, I use this often when looking for definitions at the start of a new topic to test prior learning or at the end of a lesson to assess learning.

You need sets of 3 different coloured post it notes. Let's say you have yellow, blue and pink.

Every learner is given a yellow post it. Ask the question, and without conferring with their peers, they write their response.

Allocate learners into pairs and give each pair a blue post it. Instruct the pairs to compare their answers and write a new combined one.

Now put learners into groups – at least 2 pairs per group – and give each group a pink post it. Instruct the group to compare their answers from the blue post its and compose a collaborative group answer.

Facilitate feedback as a whole group and write key words from their definitions on a flip chart.

Next show them your model answer and praise them for the key words they have given which match yours.

all learners have the opportunity to contribute and stronger learners can share their knowledge with their peers.

make sure the group is big enough for all 3 steps, alternatively...

you can reduce it to a 2 step process

Q & A, feedback, stretch and challenge, prior knowledge and understanding, structure, group work, English, differentiation, independence

prior knowledge and understanding, self, peer, communication, English, reflection and evaluation

Jigsaw – *medium and high levels*

The first time I experienced this strategy in action was during a CPD event with the great Geoff Petty. It is one of my favourite group work strategies in terms of effectiveness using a learner centred approach. I use this when I have to teach complex theory. I would never consider 'teaching' theory as a lecture so I let the learners teach each other instead.

Prepare a briefing paper for each of the sub topics so the learners know exactly what research is required.

Divide the group into sub groups. These study one section of the topic. They become 'experts' in this sub–topic.

Depending on the group, send them off to do their research using your resource centre or take reference books into the classroom. Allocate an appropriate time period to return to the classroom.

Next each sub–topic group member is given a number: 1, 2, 3, etc.

Then instruct all the 1s to reform into one group, all the 2s into another group and so on. There is then one expert from each subtopic in each new group. These new groups are called "teaching groups", and students teach other their 'expert' topic.

Now this can be very tricky the first time you do it and even more so if you don't have equal numbers in the group. Here is an example to help you:

'I want to use four groups of three students which needs 12 students but I have 14'. This doesn't matter. Make two sub–topic groups bigger by one student. Don't say who is the 'extra' student. When it comes to numbering students **you** pair up two students in each of the bigger groups to work together. Do this just before creating the 'teaching groups' (not earlier), to ensure one of the pair doesn't become a passenger. Be unpredictable about who you pair up. For a class of 14, see example following.

Sub–topic learning groups				Teaching groups
Sub topic A	1 2 3 1			1 1 1 1 1
Sub topic B	1 2 3 2			2 2 2 2 2
Sub topic C	1 2 3			3 3 3 3
Sub topic D	1 2 3			

Complete the activity by a short presentation to summarise the findings to ensure all aspects of the topic are covered.

There may be one or two sub topics that are not as complex as others so allocate the topics appropriate to the sub topic group. Where you have an 'extra' learner, make this one of your weaker learners so you can pair them with a stronger learner for the teaching group.

facilitate the research giving help and prompts to ensure all sub topic groups are engaged and progressing

feedback, stretch and challenge, differentiation, assessment, pace, structure, group work, English, independence, digital technologies

peer, communication, English , research skills, reflection and evaluation

Partners *– medium to high levels*

This is a slightly easier version of the *Jigsaw*.

The class is divided into teams of four.

Each team then subdivides into 2 sets of partners.

Each partnership is given a separate assignment/task to master or research with a view to being able to teach the other partnership.

Teams go back together with each set of partners teaching the other set.

Encourage the partners to quiz team mates and as you facilitate the 'teaching' throw in some challenging and thought provoking questions.

Complete the activity by a short presentation to summarise the findings to ensure all aspects of the topic are covered.

As a plenary of reflection and evaluation, the group reviews how well they learned and taught and how they might improve the process.

    be selective when allocating pairs and groups to ensure all learners can contribute and are appropriately supported.

    prior knowledge and understanding, Q & A, feedback, stretch and challenge, assessment, pace, structure, group work, differentiation, equality and diversity, digital technologies

![AFL]   *prior knowledge and understanding, peer, communication, linking theory to practice, reflection and evaluation*

Trade Exhibition – *medium to high levels*

This strategy was introduced to me by my brilliant colleague Gerard. It uses the *Jigsaw* principle with a new twist but if you have odd numbers, then refer to the *Jigsaw* example to help you allocate sub groups.

The class is divided into teams of between four and eight learners (preferably with an equal number in each).

Each team is given a different task or question to consider and records key points on a piece of flip chart paper. These are then pinned to the wall in different places and given a number.

Each team then splits into sub–groups, with the number of sub–groups equaling the number of teams. Sub–groups in each team are allocated a number.

Learners with the same sub–group number from each team join together and then asked to stand next to the flip chart display with that number.

The learners at each flip chart who were part of the team who prepared it then present findings to other learners.

After a set time, groups then rotate to next flip chart and the learners who prepared that one then present. Continue until each group has visited each exhibit.

 consider individual needs when allocating groups to ensure all learners can contribute and are supported

 have lots of coloured pens so they can produce visually appealing posters and tap into their creativity

prior knowledge and understanding, Q & A, feedback, stretch and challenge, assessment, pace, structure, group work, differentiation, equality and diversity

prior knowledge and understanding, peer, communication, linking theory to practice, reflection and evaluation

Spectacles – *all levels*

This is another strategy devised by Geoff Petty and great to use for case studies. This strategy can result in some very profound thinking skills being practiced.

Students are given resources and are asked to look at these with different questions in mind, or from different points of view. For example, in motor vehicle, a particular car may be under investigation but learners are grouped with 1 group looking at it from the manufacturers point of view, 1 from the mechanics point of view and 1 from the buyers point of view to discuss the merits and issues with the design , maintenance and performance of the vehicle.

Each group then feeds back and discussions are raised as each group then considers others points of view.

As always with group work consider individual needs when allocating groups to ensure all learners can contribute and are supported. You may be able to tap into the diverse knowledge of particular learners, for example, as in the illustration above, one learner may actually own that model of car

prior knowledge and understanding, Q & A, feedback, stretch and challenge, assessment, pace, structure, group work, differentiation, equality and diversity

prior knowledge and understanding, peer, communication, linking theory to practice, reflection and evaluation

Carousel – *all levels*

There is quite a lot of preparation involved with this but if you make sure you make good quality resources that you can use again then it's worth the effort. In my subject area – teacher training, there is not a lot of maths involved so I sometimes do this using maths resources. If you are teaching HE or professional programmes that don't have maths elements, it's a good filler.

Prepare tables with activities of the same theme but at different levels of complexity. In pairs or 3's depending on the size of the group, they complete each table task before moving on. Make sure you have at least 2 free tables to ensure groups don't have to wait for a free table. Include an answer sheet which is kept face down until they can't do any more.

be selective in your allocation of pairs to facilitate peer teaching and support

Make sure you make good quality resources by laminating so learners are not tempted to doodle on them and they can be used over and over again. If appropriate, provide a paper version for the learners to take with them as revision material.

prior knowledge and understanding, English, Q & A, feedback, stretch and challenge, assessment, pace, structure, group work, differentiation, equality and diversity

prior knowledge and understanding, self, peer, communication, English, linking theory to practice, reflection and evaluation

Circle View – *all levels*

This is an interesting strategy to use and can be utilized as a starter, plenary, filler or evaluation between tasks. Implemented as suggested, it also ensures the stronger/louder members of the group can't dominate. Consider the best way to integrate this into the session and whether you are using it to generate further discussion and learning

Seat the group in a circle and instruct them to talk – uninterrupted – on a particular subject which seeks their opinion. Be firm that while they are talking, everyone must listen and not interrupt nor contradict the speakers opinion. Make sure you allocate the same amount of time for everyone. Do allow learners to pass if they need more thinking time but don't forget to come back to them at the end. For example, in an art class, you might ask the question – 'What is your favourite art movement and why?' In beauty therapy 'What is the best cosmetic range and why?'.

This strategy gives weaker learners the confidence to speak in the knowledge they won't be interrupted and they can share their opinions in a safe and structured environment. Hopefully, all learners will learn something new about something they knew little about.

feedback, prior knowledge and understanding, structure, English, differentiation, equality and diversity, independence

prior knowledge and understanding, peer, self, employability, communication, English, critical thinking skills, reflection and evaluation

Spy in the Camp *– all levels*

A big and dare I say lazy mistake to make is setting each table group the same task. When it comes to feedback, I always feel sorry for the last group to present as it has been done 2 or 3 times before and the whole feedback gets very boring. However, if you do need them to do the same task you can add a sense of fun by employing spies.

Select a spy or ask each table group to select one who will visit other groups to see what they are doing and listen in on their conversations. They can then report back to their own group to enhance their progress. Remember to always facilitate group work using stretch and challenge questioning techniques.

if you are allocating the spy, don't be tempted to select the strongest group member. This could be the opportunity for a weaker or less confident member to take on a responsible role.

Q & A, feedback, stretch and challenge, pace, structure, group work*

peer, communication*

* you may recognise and add more key indicators and assessment being met depending on the topic

Silent Praise – *all levels (see also Workshops)*

This is a good strategy to use if you don't really want to interrupt group work as they are clearly focussed and on task but you know you should be doing something. Listen and watch attentively and when you see some really good practice or hear something fabulous, write your praise on a post it and quietly put it in front of the learner. This is a great motivator without embarrassing anyone who might not take praise easily.

 depending on the group, you could just make notes and feed back at the end.

 if the group is fairly small, you should be able to think of something for each learner so they are all praised by the end of the lesson

 feedback, assessment, equality and diversity

 self, peer, communication, reflection and evaluation

Group/Pair selection Techniques – *all levels*

Sometimes you may just want to create random groups or pairs and need to quickly select them. You can have a bit more fun than simply choosing randomly. Here are a few you might want to try.

Biggest/smallest

Hands

Feet

Ears

Noses

Birth dates

Month

Year

Day

Longest/shortest/tallest

Hair

Nails

Height

Wearing

Most colours

Least colours

Jewellery

Most/least

Brothers

Sisters

Sons/daughters

Pets

Colour

Eyes

Skin

Owns a...

Cat

Dog

Car

Playing Card Selection Techniques

A simple pack of playing cards can be a great resource to help facilitate a random group selection. There are a variety of ways of using the cards to create groups of 4:

Fan out the cards face down and ask learners to select one, learners then group with other with the same number. You can then regroup by asking them to group themselves into same suit groups.

Use the King, Queen, Jack and Ace and allocate roles for each suit.

To embed maths:

❖ ask learners to line up in number order

❖ ask learners to group into even and odd numbers

❖ when teaching mean, median, mode, learners are already in groups, randomly select numbers and use those to make calculations

Group Presentations

Many group work tasks culminate in group presentations. This gives our learners valuable skills, raises confidence, improves communication skills, develops IT skills and can add valuable evidence for assessment.

Think about how you can vary how these are undertaken using the strategies below.

Random Objects – *all levels*

You can also add a sense of fun and develop creative thinking skills by including some unusual objects. For example, fill a small table with random objects such as toys or household objects and invite them to choose one object which they can build into their presentation. It doesn't matter if the link is rather tenuous, the point is you have made them think creatively – a valuable transferrable skill.

   learners are given a choice

   stretch and challenge, differentiation, equality and diversity

   creative thinking skills

Question Time – all levels

Some learners may not be as attentive as they should when others are presenting so here is one way to keep them all focussed and attentive. Let them know that at any point during the presentation, you are going to stop it and you will pick one learner in the audience to ask a question of the presenters. It's worked for me, even with the most chatty groups.

you may need to prompt some learners if they can't think of a question

Q & A, stretch and challenge, assessment, pace, structure, independence

peer, communication, reflection and evaluation

Peer Assessment – *all levels*

Another way to keep everyone listening and watching is to provide a grid with agreed criteria for them to peer assess each presentation. Keep it simple and related to the presentation and not the topic such as communication and visual effectiveness. The feedback could be a score out of ten or a written assessment depending on the level. For higher level learners, you could also include feedback on the topic if they have enough information to make a judgement.

you might want to have some grids relating to presentation skills and some on topic content and allocate appropriately according to level and ability

feedback, assessment, structure, target setting, differentiation, English, independence

self, peer, communication, English, reflection and evaluation

As seen on TV – *middle to high levels*

Task the groups to present in the style of a TV show. You can give prizes if the audience can guess the show. This is perfect for performing arts students.

 this may be an opportunity for quieter learners to shine as they may be adept at drama

 this is great fun and results in a lot of hilarity which may take the focus away from the topics so be careful to only use this strategy at an appropriate time

stretch and challenge, group work, equality and diversity

communication

*See also Carousel **and** Trade Exhibition in **Group Work***

Chapter 5 — Assessment For Learning

Note it is assessment *for* learning and not *of* learning. The emphasis is on learning from something and not just passing a test or exam. The majority of the activities in this toolkit are for formative assessment purposes although some can be used as summative evidence therefore it's important they have value in terms of generating and building on learning ahead of any final work that needs to be achieved. The following are a collection of activities ranging from simple to more complex which I hope will inspire you to be creative and play around with to contextualise for you and your learners' needs.

Matching Games *– all levels*

This requires some preparation but is certainly worth the effort as you can use them over and over again. The most simple form is to prepare cards with, for example, a key word or phrase and another card with a definition or answer on. Learners need to match the cards.

You could use this to test prior knowledge at the beginning of the lesson and repeat at the end to assess learning; at the end of a topic; within a session before moving on which also acts as a breather in a theory lesson.

This can be done as a table activity or using Velcro as a wall activity.

If it's quite complex, you could instruct learners to change tables or assess others tables during the activity to support learning. Use a timer tool for this to add pace.

You could provide key words and only some of the answers with blank cards for them to complete.

In vocational subjects, you could use pictures for the clues instead, for example tools used for specific tasks.

Make sure your groups are selected to address differentiation to ensure everyone engages. Facilitate by questioning during the activity to support and challenge. Some tables could have complete sets while other sets with some blank cards depending on ability

 laminate the cards so you can use them again and provide fine point dry wipe pens if you are using the blank cards strategy so they can be cleaned for the next time

 Q & A, feedback, prior knowledge and understanding, assessment, pace, structure, stretch and challenge, group work, English, differentiation, digital technologies

prior knowledge and understanding, self, peer, communication, English, linking theory to practice

Terminology Bingo – *all levels*

Create a bingo type grid with key words on which learners have to cross off when they are mentioned in the lesson. At the end of the lesson, for a plenary, learners have to write a definition of the word or create a sentence with the word in depending on the level and time available.. Alternatively, the plenary can be turned into a starter at the beginning of the next lesson.

 you can provide different words or plenary tasks for the different levels – some learners write a definition, some write a sentence

 laminate the cards so you can use them again and provide fine point dry wipe pens so they can be cleaned for the next time.

 be careful the activity doesn't detract from the lesson in progress. This may be better used during a demonstration with some learners.

feedback, stretch and challenge, assessment, pace, structure, English, differentiation, independence

 self, communication, English

I am..... – *all levels*

If your subject includes something that includes a series of steps or sequence whether it's practical or theoretical, this is a fun way to consolidate learning or even use as a prior learning starter or evaluating learning plenary.

Create labels with steps on and stick on learners. They then have to get into sequence then each one in turn describes who/what they are, and their main purpose or how they work.

you can select which learner gets which label to ensure everyone can contribute and others are challenged

Q & A, feedback, stretch and challenge, prior knowledge and understanding, assessment, structure, group work, independence

self, peer, communication, English, linking theory to practice, employability, reflection and evaluation

Key Word Game (Verbosity) – *all levels*

One of our favourite games at family parties is playing Verbosity. Put the class into 2 teams and provide a variety of cards with key words on them. Each team member has to describe the word without saying it and their team have to guess what it is. Make sure you have a timer and if its not guessed at the end of time the other team can guess to steal their point.

If you have the time you can advance the cards by having 3 different levels of key words per card worth different levels of points so they can start with the lower numbers and work up to the higher numbers (you won't have to make so many cards either). You could use pictures as well as or instead of words.

Q & A, feedback, prior knowledge and understanding, stretch and challenge, assessment, pace, structure, group work, English, differentiation

prior knowledge and understanding, peer, communication, English

Case Studies *– all levels*

One of the best ways to bring the real world into the classroom is through case studies. These also help to develop your learners problem solving skills which is a vital skill in the workplace.

Case studies are very subject specific so you need to decide what type you use. For example you could ask:

What happens next? – provide a scenario with the end missing.

What would you do? – provide a case study – preferably from a real situation – and ask them what they would do.

What questions do you need to ask? – provide a case study where they need to make a decision based on information they don't yet have so they formulate a series of questions that need to be asked and of whom.

Who else should be involved? – for example teaching safeguarding from a case study or a restaurant customer with an allergy.

You could do this as a carousel – see page 74.

pair or group learners to support and/or challenge with different case studies

Q & A, prior knowledge and understanding, feedback, stretch and challenge, assessment, pace, structure, English, maths (if it includes statistics) differentiation, equality and diversity, independence

prior knowledge and understanding, self, peer, employability, English, problem solving, critical thinking, linking theory to practice, reflection and evaluation

Odd One Out – *low to medium levels*

Before a practical activity, set out the tools or materials to be used but add one that is not required. Learners have to guess which one is the odd one out. To advance this further, use direct questioning to ask learners what each tool is and what it's used for. Include any health and safety considerations where appropriate.

using direct questioning is a great way to address differentiation

Q & A, prior knowledge and understanding, feedback, stretch and challenge, assessment, pace, structure, English, maths (if it includes statistics) differentiation, equality and diversity

prior knowledge and understanding, self, peer, employability, English, linking theory to practice reflection and evaluation

Play Your Cards Right – *all levels*

Create A4 laminated playing cards and use the concept of play your cards right. When learners get a question right they have the chance to play. Take it one further by putting questions on the cards which they have to answer correctly to proceed.

 you could allow each learner to ask for a clue but only once in the session

 it's unlikely you will have a shelf to play the game so you could use velcro so they stick on the wall

 stretch and challenge, assessment, Q & A, feedback, structure, pace, differentiation, equality and diversity, maths, prior knowledge and understanding

prior knowledge and understanding, self, maths, communication, linking theory to practice

Teach and Listen – *all levels*

This is good for classes of chatty students as you give them permission to talk. It's also a good way to train them how to listen too!

At appropriate points in the lesson, in pairs, give them a number 1 and 2. When you say 'one teach', number 1's explain whatever point has been made in the lesson and importantly number 2's can only listen. Keep it short – one or two minutes, then continue with the lesson. Next time, 2's teach and 1's listen. This is also a handy plenary if you have a spare 5 minutes at the end of the lesson.

Pair a strong learner with a weaker one. The strong learner is more likely to use a reader friendly explanation which is helpful to the weaker learner.

feedback, prior knowledge and understanding, stretch and challenge, assessment, pace, structure, group work , English, differentiation, independence

prior knowledge and understanding, self, peer, communication, English, linking theory to practice, reflection and evaluation

Read All About It – *middle to high levels*

As the lesson progresses, create a graffiti wall with newspaper headlines which the learners create themselves. This will help them remember important points made. For example, in Hair and Beauty, when learning about the skin layers, the headline could be 'Shocking Discovery! Epidermis is found on top of Dermis! '.

 If you have an interactive whiteboard, you can save it and upload to your VLE. Alternatively, do it on a large piece of paper so it can be displayed. I buy wallpaper lining and cut off what I need, as flip chart paper is never big enough.

 make sure everyone has the opportunity to create a headline. Use gifted learners skills to create a visually effective design

 stretch and challenge, assessment, group work, English, equality and diversity

 peer, communication, English, linking theory to practice, creativity

Anonymous Questions – *all levels*

Quite often, some learners are too shy or nervous to ask questions during a session or don't want others to know they don't understand something. If your session involves a break at some point, ask them to write a question they need answering or a further clarification on something they are struggling with. Learners put them in a box as they leave and you can use the break to sort through and spend the beginning of the second half addressing the issues. This will also give you a good idea how learning is progressing.

As the question is anonymous, weaker learners have a safe environment to ask questions. Stronger learners also get the opportunity to answer the questions

Q & A, prior knowledge and understanding, feedback, assessment, stretch and challenge, structure, pace, differentiation, equality and diversity

prior knowledge and understanding, self, communication, English, reflection and evaluation

Assessment Practice – *middle to high levels*

This is particularly useful where work is going to be graded to give learners a better idea of what is expected of them.

Give learners an exemplar piece of work and the criteria that it was being assessed against. Ask learners to mark the work and give it a grade. You can then ask them what their grade was and explain how they came to that judgement. You can then share the given grade and explain how the judgement was made.

 If you have the time, use 2 exemplars to show different grades e.g. a pass and a distinction level. If you don't have time, split the class in half and give them different graded papers. Where appropriate, ask them to identify any spelling or grammar errors.

 if you split the class in half, make sure it's a mix of abilities to allow the weaker learners to see what higher level work looks like

 Q & A, feedback, prior knowledge and understanding, stretch and challenge, assessment, structure, group work, target setting, English, differentiation

prior knowledge and understanding, self, peer, communication, English, reflection and evaluation

Learner Devised Revision – *middle to high levels*

It's always tempting to give out past papers for revision lessons which I always thought were boring. So turn it around and get the learners to devise their own questions to answer. You could give them a text that is to be learned and they devise their own questions. The text is then put away and they then compose their answers.

this allows individuals to work on their own perceived weaknesses rather than everyone doing the same regardless of ability

prior knowledge and understanding, Q & A, feedback, stretch and challenge, assessment, structure, target setting, English, differentiation, equality and diversity, independence

self, prior knowledge and understanding, English, linking theory to practice, problem solving skills, reflection and evaluation

Picture This *– all levels*

Turn text into pictures as a visual representation of what is being learned.

This can be done during the lesson or at the end. Ask learners to draw what is being learned either as an image or a cartoon depending on how artistic they are.

This can be extended into a graphic organiser format such as a flow chart to show progression and links to learning.

 this will appeal to the visual learners in your group

 refer to my tip of using wallpaper lining so you have a nice big canvas to work on

 prior knowledge and understanding, feedback, stretch and challenge, assessment, structure, group work, differentiation, equality and diversity

prior knowledge and understanding, peer, creativity,

Mini Whiteboard Q & A – *all levels*

A fun and different way to do Q & A, put learners into pairs or 3's and instruct to write their answers on the whiteboard. Ensure you give a specific time to answer – from 5 to 30 seconds depending on the complexity of the answer – then everyone holds up their boards at the same time. This will make sure no one cheats by changing their answer. You can keep a tally of their correct answers on a board and give a prize at the end.

 Mix up the pairs but make sure everyone engages and the stronger learner doesn't take over. However, it will give weaker learners confidence and a sense of achievement if they are on a winning team.

 Mini whiteboards can be expensive to purchase so an easy option is to laminate plain paper to use instead. I use this but also during a game of snakes and ladders – see page 98 following.

remember to use dry wipe pens and provide a mini rubber or cloth to wipe clean

Q & A, feedback, prior knowledge and understanding, stretch and challenge, assessment, pace, structure, group work, English

prior knowledge and understanding, self, peer, communication, English, linking theory to practice, reflection and evaluation

Snakes and Ladders – *all levels*

I play this at least once with each of my groups. It's great fun, very competitive and it's also the luck of the dice that can result in a winner so it's fair for everyone. You will need a snakes and ladders template and enough dice for each sub group to have 2.

I do this as a revision before moving onto a new topic, so devise at least 10 questions and be sure to start with a few easy ones so everyone has a chance to throw the dice and move around the board. Using the mini whiteboards, use the same strategy as 'mini whiteboard Q & A' to make sure there is no cheating. The purpose of having 2 dice is if you think part of the answer is right you can allow them to throw one dice so you can reward nearly right answers.

Give the instruction that each member of the group take it in turns to write the answers down. As the throw of the dice adds an element of chance, everyone has the opportunity to win.

Use the concept of Bloom's taxonomy to structure your questions to add challenge but do throw an easy one in again towards the end or you may find some groups get frustrated if they are struggling. You could extend this if time allows by going back over the answers and promoting discussion. Don't do this in the middle of the game or it will diffuse the fun element.

Q & A, feedback, prior knowledge and understanding, stretch and challenge, assessment, pace, structure, group work, English, equality and diversity

prior knowledge and understanding, self, peer, communication, English, linking theory to practice, reflection and evaluation

Question Jenga – *all levels*

I expect most of you will know the Jenga game. It's fun and challenging as a game itself, now all you need to do is stick questions on the pieces and learners take turns sliding a piece out and answering the questions. There are a multitude of ways to use this in a lesson and some are suggested here:

❖ As a starter or plenary, learners take turns coming to the table to take a piece – you decide how they are chosen – and they ask the class or an individual of their or your choice to answer

❖ Use it as a brain break during a long session to add variety

❖ Use it for behaviour management, anyone needing a prompt to behave has to come up and take a piece then answer it

❖ You can use it to embed maths by having calculations on the pieces

❖ Or one of your own creative ideas!

 once the question has been asked you can decide who should answer based on the level of question

make sure the same person isn't asked more than once. Think about what you will do should the tower fall

Q & A, feedback, prior knowledge and understanding, stretch and challenge, assessment, pace, structure, group work, English, maths, equality and diversity

prior knowledge and understanding, self, peer, communication, English, maths, linking theory to practice, reflection and evaluation

Number Crunching *– lower levels*

This is a great idea for a starter, plenary, filler or to embed maths.

Prepare a range of random numbers and give them out or allow them to select blindly. Then task them to come up with a calculation that includes that number. There are so many ways this can be varied to suit the purpose so here are some suggestions:

Also prepare some mathematical symbols which they also select and have to use.

The number card used must be the answer – the calculation the learner has created is solved by the group then they reveal the answer card.

Pair up learners who have to combine their number cards.

Put in 4's and include 2 symbols they have to use.

You decide how the cards are allocated. You are then able to give specific cards to individuals in order to differentiate in terms of complexity

stretch and challenge, assessment, group work, maths, differentiation, equality and diversity

self, peer, maths

Sock it to me – *middle to high levels*

This fabulous activity was generated by one of my student teachers in art to enable students to develop their skills in drawing shape and texture. However, it can be used to help learners fine tune their language skills as they need to find the right descriptive words.

You'll need to purchase some socks – use your local market for cheap ones but not too thin that they can be seen through. Then rummage in those drawers, you know the ones we all have that contain all those random objects we never use from one day to the next. Place an object in each sock and ask learners to select one at random. For the art class, the learners place their non drawing hand into the sock then draw what they can feel. The fact that they can't see the object helps them to 'see' the texture in a different manner.

For non-art classes, they need to describe what they feel using a range of descriptive words.

 you could choose to allocate specific objects to either support or challenge individual learners

 It's a good idea to try to use objects that are not easy to guess such as dice or keys otherwise it will interfere with the creative process. Have a look in the garden for unusual stones or foliage or something that is broken as long as there are no sharp parts.

most importantly, ensure there are no parts of the object that could injure them.

Q & A, feedback, stretch and challenge, assessment, English, differentiation, independence

self, communication, English, creative thinking, reflection and evaluation

Table Graffiti – *all levels*

If you are up for taking a risk then this one is for you. The idea came from a student school teacher who was faced with a difficult and challenging group who didn't like to write as they said it was boring.

Clear the desks and give out dry wipe pens to all learners. Then instruct them to write their ideas, drafts, thoughts on the desks, whatever is related to the topic. Even the most reluctant learner will enjoy the novelty of doing something that is usually a disciplinary offence! They can rub out incorrect work which gives them more freedom to experiment with their literacy skills. They can then copy into their books or worksheets.

It's easier for the weaker learners to see others work which supports their learning. Every learner will be keen to engage.

You know your own learners and will therefore be selective who to try this with. Make sure ground rules for this activity are set. Test out the desks beforehand to make sure it will rub out completely.

Q & A, feedback, assessment, structure, group work, English, differentiation, equality and diversity, prior knowledge and understanding, independence

prior knowledge and understanding, peer, self, communication, English, linking theory to practice, reflection and evaluation

Chapter 6 – Demonstrations

If you are teaching a practical skill then you will be conducting lots of demonstrations. For most vocational teachers, this is where they are most comfortable, showing skills they have perfected after many years in industry. For learners too, this is their favourite part of going to college or university, but for them it's the doing rather than the watching so you need to make the demonstration as interactive as you can. Demonstrations are no fun for anybody if they are:

❖ Too long

❖ Boring, having nothing to do but watch

❖ Too complicated to remember in one go

❖ Rushed

❖ Badly executed

You don't want to provide opportunities for learners to chat to each other off topic or check their phones while you are enjoying yourself doing your stuff!

There are many strategies, resources and activities that you can use to make learning from a demonstration more memorable and interactive. When planning a demonstration, also plan to check if learning is taking place, check learners are focussed and check whether they can replicate the practice safely and correctly.

So you need to plan:

❖ What questions you are going to ask at what point

❖ Is the demonstration going to be split into separate sections?

❖ Do you or the learners need to compose a step by step list?

❖ How are you going to involve the learners in the demonstration?

❖ Will everyone be able to see?

If you have a big group you may have to split it into separate demonstrations so have something ready for those not watching at that time – a work sheet, a risk assessment to complete or preparing their area for working by getting tools/materials.

Work sheets – *all levels*

These are a handy way for learners to produce their own resources for when they are carrying out their practical or as revision material. You need to provide a proforma for them as you can't be sure they will make the correct or enough notes for themselves.

A gapped handout is always useful but do make sure you have one beside you too so you can direct them to it at the appropriate moments.

Alternatively, you could provide a table format with the steps down the first column, a second column for 'how to' and a third with 'important considerations. This will help you to formulate the questions you are going to ask.

 you can make different worksheets depending on levels and ability

Q & A, feedback, assessment, pace, structure, target setting, independence

self, linking theory to practice, reflection and evaluation

Questioning – *all levels*

If you don't want your learners distracted by filling in work sheets during the demonstration, you can use whole group and direct Q & A which is also an opportunity to check attention and add challenge. Typically, questions could follow this method:

Who has done this before? Followed by, 'what do you find tricky/easy when doing this'?

Then using direct or group method:

What should I do first? (this could be related to health and safety)

Why?

What should I do next?

Why?

What if.....?

What else could I do if....?

What else could I use this tool/product/resource for?

Some of the questions are simple or factual while the challenging ones require more analytical thinking skills. Firing these out constantly using direct Q & A keeps everyone on their toes.

 you can direct your questions to specific learners to both support and challenge

Q & A, feedback, stretch and challenge, assessment, pace, structure, differentiation, equality and diversity, prior knowledge and understanding

prior knowledge and understanding, self, peer, employability, communication, linking theory to practice, reflection and evaluation

Using learners as a resource – *all levels*

Health and safety allowing and if the procedure is fairly simple, you could use the learners in turn to demonstrate while you talk them through it. Better still, have the procedure as a handout and ask the learners in turn to talk whoever is on the hot spot through it.

If you do have a learner who already has some of the required skills, then let them do the demonstration so you can concentrate on making it interactive. Using learners' skills for peer teaching is a great motivator to influence learners to learn and practice outside the classroom.

do make sure you use direct Q & A to ensure everyone is involved and keep everyone focussed

stretch and challenge, assessment, Q & A, feedback, structure, pace, differentiation, equality and diversity

employability, communication, linking theory to practice

Chapter 7 — Workshops

Workshops are a great opportunity to help learners develop their time management and employability skills by building up to commercial timings.

One thing that I don't like to see when observing practical sessions is when a teacher does it for them. You really do need to resist the temptation to take over when they are struggling. You should be able to talk them through it slowly. Remember, you won't always be there to help out when they are stuck or things go wrong when they are out there in industry.

Workshops turn the teacher into a facilitator but we must remember that this is a learning environment so it's not good practice to just let them get on with it while you have a wander round nodding your head or even getting on with some marking.

You need to continue to check if learning is taking place and to continue to guide and challenge to keep learners busy, on track in terms of their personal learning goals and the objectives set for the session and ensure every learner achieves.

Traffic Light Facilitator tools – all levels

It's not easy to facilitate smartly when you have big groups or large work spaces such as can be found within construction. A great resource to help you do this is using the traffic light system.

In a classroom, coloured cups can be used by the learners to indicate the type and level of help they need:

In a large construction workshop, hair and beauty salon or art studio, you could make small coloured smiley faces from laminated paper, string them together and hang them next to the work station:

If the red cup or smiley is showing then the learner is stuck and needs help right away so they can continue.

If the amber is showing, they have a quick question but can continue while they wait for you.

If the green is showing, they are happy and confident to continue.

It is vital, though, that you don't ignore the greens; take time out to praise or ask a question so they don't feel left out and you still check learning is taking place.

Using these resources will help you to circulate smartly and keep everyone busy and on track.

Starting the session – *all levels*

All workshops including those continuing after a lunch break should have a structured start. Its all too easy to allow the students to wander in willy-nilly, gather their resources, don their PPI and continue with a task. You and they need to know where they are up to, what their short and long term targets are, and what your expectations for the day are. It's your opportunity to link learning to assessment, employability and achievement.

For the first session of the day, start with everyone gathered around and choose to ask one or more of:

- ❖ Have you been able to use learning from the previous session and what did you do?

- ❖ What do you need to practice more today?

- ❖ Do you need me to demonstrate or explain anything again?

- ❖ What is your personal target today?

- ❖ What are the specific health and safety considerations when carrying out these tasks?

- ❖ If you are continuing after a long break such as lunch, start with everyone gathered around and choose to ask one or more of:

- ❖ Tell me one thing you found tricky and one thing you found easy this morning?

- ❖ What do you need to practice more this afternoon?

- ❖ Do you need me to demonstrate or explain anything again?

- ❖ What do you want to perfect by the end of today?

I'm sure you can think of plenty more questions and particularly subject specific as a recap.

Self directed learning – *middle to high levels*

In some areas such as Art and Design, learners may be working on long term projects. A brilliant resource one of my student teachers used was to help learners set their own objectives for that particular session. Its such a simple but very effective resource which also helped her to facilitate – she could see clearly where the learner was up to and what they were doing.

An example of the proforma for a 2 hour session is shown below:

Name

Project

Objective 1

Objective 2

Objective 3

Objective 4

and a completed one looks like this

Name   Jane Jones

Project   Season's sculpture

Objective 1 collect final materials and cut to length

Objective 2 attach and glaze

Objective 3   complete annotation while waiting to dry

Objective 4 check process and adjust where appropriate. Clear away.

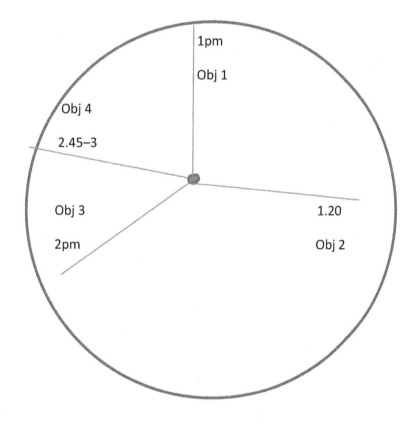

learners are given the opportunity to set their own pace

 feedback, Q & A, assessment, pace, structure, target setting, maths, differentiation, equality and diversity, independence

 self, employability, reflection and evaluation

Linking theory and practice

Invariably vocational learners love the workshop and dislike the classroom, so why do we insist on only teaching theory in the classroom? You're on the back foot as soon as you enter the classroom so bring the theory into the workshop, and where possible, the workshop into the classroom. If you can bring equipment used in the workshop into the classroom learners can touch and practice as well as see what they are learning about rather than a picture on the white board.

I expect your Q & A in the workshop is related to theory as well as the practical questions but one of the best examples I've seen is as the picture below shows. Ron, a painting and decorating tutor is quite the artist and this is just a small example of his artwork in his workshop.

Ron's rationale is that while his learners are waiting for paint or paper to dry, they can go to the wall and answer the questions. It's also a visually appealing display with fun cartoons and certainly for me, has the wow factor.

It can be rather difficult to have pieces of paper and files around a workshop so make use of any white boards you have to display targets for the session. Construction workshops can make good use of theirs and provides structure.

An added feature of using this strategy is that learners themselves record their achievement and next goal so they take more ownership of their learning and progress.

 Of course the teacher needs to record all this so the easiest way is to take a photo of it at the end of the session and it can then be transferred to the usual electronic records.

Where appropriate, build in peer assessment as its always inspiring for learners to receive praise from their peers as well as the teacher. If they have done something particularly well, they can share this with their peers. A good reward for the more committed learners.

If one of the more able learners finishes early, as an extension activity, you can ask them to engage in peer teaching to support the less able learner.   Again, a good reward for their dedication.

You also need a structured end to the session. Often, they end by everyone clearing away and wandering off when they're done. As at the beginning of the session, you need a structured end. This is where learners have the opportunity the articulate what they have learned and gives you the opportunity to praise them as a group and talk about next steps to enthuse them for the next session. Have a look at the plenary chapter for ideas.

Music in the classroom/workshop

Music during learning is somewhat contentious not least because in most institutions mobile phones are not allowed to be used for obvious reasons. As most music is stored on phones, learners like to plug themselves in and listen privately. Some say it helps them learn and they are probably right in some instances but we then have the issue of what they are listening to, the irritation for others to have to listen to muted sounds coming from the person next to them, and of course the temptation to have a little peek at their social networks.

A simple answer to the problem is for you to choose the music. In a beauty salon practical, they usually have a good selection of suitably relaxing tunes to create an ambient mood and to avoid therapists and clients alike having a singalong as they are always instrumental. So of you are going to play music while students are doing theoretical work, then instrumental is the way to go. For a lively practical workshop, suitable lyrical music could be used but be prepared for budding X Factor contestants to show their talent!

Some interesting research has been done about music for learning which is worth having a look at. I've included a couple of books by Chris Brewer and recommend his article on the John Hopkins School of Education website in the reading list. Brewer bases his conclusions on extensive research and suggests that music can influence attention, attitude and the atmosphere. For example, if you have a boisterous group, try playing some calming music as they walk into the classroom, it's amazing to see how it calms them down quite quickly. The influence of music on our mood can be quite dramatic as it stimulates emotions, so have a go and see what happens. You could even choose a track that links with the content of the session, for example *'Leaving on a Jet Plane'* for travel and tourism or money songs for business and finance/accounting. To include a learning point, you could choose a song linked to the session and ask learners to guess what the session is about.

Choose wisely and it could make a difference.

Chapter 8 – Digital Technologies for Teaching, Learning & Assessment

Author Sarah Grisbrook

Edited by Joanna Smithies

Digital technology has been creeping up on us for many years now and I think that its fair to say that most professionals have dabbled with it in many different ways, however the UK further education sector is now recognising the importance of technology for learning as a way of engaging learners and influencing and enhancing the learning outcomes as well as improving teaching and learning.

With the provision of further education becoming more competitive, it is important to provide students with an experience that incorporates the use of innovative technology by doing this we are preparing our learners for employment and providing them with the skill needs of tomorrow.

You may already be familiar with the FELTAG report which makes recommendations to the government to make necessary funding and policy changes in order to cater for the Digital Age.

In response to this report, the Government, OFSTED and the SFA have all taken this on board and as a result investments have already been made by improving JANET to enable a fast and effective service to educational providers to cater for the digital age. Consultations are currently taking place in terms of funding mechanisms and how OFSTED make judgments on the impact of Digital Technologies for teaching and learning.

This chapter will give you a taster of strategies that you can be using to enhance and prepare our learners for the digital age, but before we start I think it's only fair that we address a few important factors.

Preparing your learners

How many times have you heard someone say, " the kids of today know how to use technology better than I do"; I expect 9 times out of 10 this is right. We see the younger generation using mobile phones, tablets, iPads and computers most of the time, in fact they rarely have one out of their hand. However if you looked carefully at what they are looking at you will see that most are engaging with social media such as: Facebook, Twitter, Instagram, Snap chat, Youtube or just plain old texting and messaging. Before engaging with any technology I would say consult with your learners about what technology they are using and how they are using it, this will give you a starting point. By embracing the diverse range of skills and experiences of your learners lessons are enriched and enjoyable and take on a more personal flavour.

As discussed earlier, learners do pick up technology quickly, but the question is do they know how to use it for learning? Will they know how to use it when they go into employment? Will they know how to use it constructively or even appropriately? Do they think about how employers can research them before they have even met them? This leads nicely to ESafety. These are the guidelines that you need to consider when thinking about using technology. These are complimentary to the Safeguarding agenda and must be considered when planning using digital media.

Technology will engage our learners and make the lesson more current, innovative and dynamic but remember my advice on adding fun with no purpose. Consider what skills are they actually going to gain from using this piece of technology; what are they going to learn which will have an impact on their future skills and development.

Some of the key digital technology skills you could consider when you are planning to use technology may include:
- Presentation skills
- Web skills
- Search skills
- Digital research skills
- Reflective skills
- Independent study skills
- Collaboration
- Peer assessment and sharing
- ESafety

As professionals it's important to keep up–to–date with modern day learning and start to take full advantage of digital technologies to equip the next generation with the tools to meet the challenges of the future workforce and boost the UK economy.

This section will give you examples of activities and resources that you could use to enrich the learning experience. In the following pages I have listed lots of different examples of technology that you could implement into your everyday teaching practice, detailing what it is and how it can be used to hit those key indicators that observers look for when observing your teaching and learning.

Smartboards

If you are lucky enough to have a Smartboard in your organisation then this section will provide you with ideas and suggestions on how to use it effectively. When I say effectively I mean it in the broadest sense of the word. The cost and maintenance of this resource is far too high for you to just use it as a Powerpoint display device, it should be used as it was intended, as an interactive technical resource. For example, your learners should be up at the board touching and moving things around. Although there has not been any concrete evidence as to whether this has an impact on learning, it nevertheless brings a fun element to the classroom environment which inevitably leads to engaged learners.

I love the Smart Notebook software, in fact so much so I have stopped using Powerpoint with my younger learners. This software allows you to create your whole lesson plan throughout, you can imbed your aims, objectives, a mind map for a recap or even an activity and then embed task instructions, timers and interactive tools and games.

WARNING

If your learners are reluctant to get up to the board use it initially as a fun tool, create some games so that they can start to build their confidence with the new technology. Learners will be resistant to engage initially if they feel challenged or put on the spot. Assure them that this device is fun but also that it brings value and purpose to their learning objectives.

Smart tools

The Smart Notebook software has some great interactive tools located in the gallery, which I have detailed below, think about using these to pose key questions either as a starter, plenary or even throughout the lesson just to make sure learning is taking place.

Keyword Dice *– all levels*

This is a quick and easy tool for recap or a summary. It's a dynamic dice which can be populated with your own keywords, once touched on the board it rolls the dice and displays a word. Once displayed the buzz begins; what does this word mean? what did we learn about it last week? how can this be used? Think about getting your learners up to hit the dice and then use the blank area on the page to record feedback, if your learners are really confident with the board get them to record the feedback on the board.

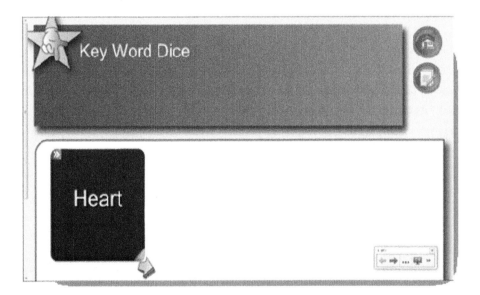

All learners can take the opportunity to 'roll the dice' depending on the size of the class. Stronger learners can be selected to record feedback.

 you could use your learner names resource – lollipop sticks, names out of a hat, to select who answers the questions

 Q & A, feedback, stretch and challenge, assessment, pace, structure, English, differentiation, prior knowledge and understanding, digital technology

prior knowledge and understanding, self, peer, English, linking theory to practice, reflection and evaluation

Random Word Generator *– all levels*

This is similar to Keyword Dice however, it allows you to have more than 6 words, again by populating it with your own words the generator will randomly display them, you can then start your activity.

 you can direct your questions to specific learners based on their level

 Q & A, feedback, stretch and challenge, assessment, pace, structure, English, differentiation, prior knowledge and understanding, digital technology

prior knowledge and understanding, self, peer, English, linking theory to practice, reflection and evaluation

Question Flippers – *all levels*

These are square blocks that allow you to insert a question, its dynamic so when you hit the block it presents a question.

 I like to use these for group work, by putting 2 or 3 on the board you can issue a question to each group and record the feedback at the side

 select your groups by differentiating abilities and allocate roles

 Q & A, feedback, stretch and challenge, assessment, pace, structure, English, differentiation, prior knowledge and understanding, digital technology

prior knowledge and understanding, self, peer, English, linking theory to practice, reflection and evaluation

Random Group Picker – *all levels*

A tool which allows you to input all class names and then the generator forms the groups for you based on the number of groups you require. This is a great way of very quickly pulling together groups for any classroom activities.

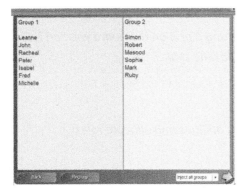

note this does not take into consideration differentiation but great for just a quick random group selection

digital technology

Timers – *all levels*

Timers are a great way of adding pace and structure to your lessons and it keeps you and your learners on track. I like to have these visible on the screen so that the learners can see them and also add sound so that it brings the activity to an immediate halt.

 this can be found in the Smart Notebook software under lesson activity toolkit within the Gallery

pace, structure, digital technology

The following tools are simple to create, you can populate them with your own keywords and away you go.

Games and Quizzes in the Smart Notebook

The Smart Notebook software has a collection of templates to create quizzes and games such as:

- Multichoice quiz
- Anagram game
- Pairs
- Keyword match
- Category sorts

and many more to choose from.

It's worth investigating the folder as there is a wealth of templates and they are very simple to use, by clicking on the edit buttons you can customise them as you wish.

Perfect for starters or summaries. You populate and customise the template to suit your subject and get the room buzzing with good question and answering.

Q & A, feedback, stretch and challenge, assessment, pace, structure, English, differentiation, prior knowledge and understanding, digital technology

prior knowledge and understanding, self, peer, English, linking theory to practice, reflection and evaluation

Smart Notebook and MS Office for visual target setting – *low to middle levels*

This works well for younger learners and works especially well for assignment workshops. This involves 2 separate resources one which is made on word and is basically a record sheet of the date, task to complete, lesson target and lesson stretch target. See below:

Date	Task to complete	Lesson target	Lesson stretch target

The learners have these visible throughout the lesson, you could even go one step further and put your aims and objectives on the reverse of the sheet so learners are aware of the lesson focus.

Resource two is a visual display to be displayed on the board, Smart Notebook software is perfect for this as they can move their own names around the board. See following image and notes:

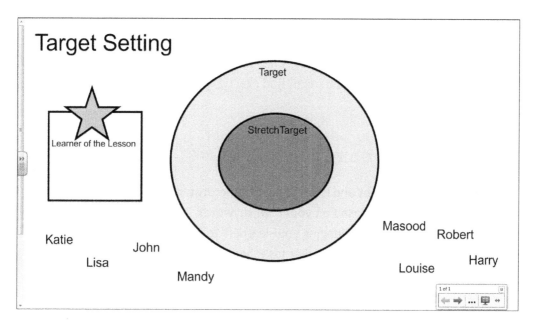

This resource is created using shapes and text boxes, this is visible on the board throughout the lesson and as learners hit their target or stretch target they can move their name into the target area. The competitiveness of this resource is a good motivator for learners. At the end of the lesson when you do your final summary of targets you can evaluate who you think has gone over and above their agreed target and excelled and then move that person of persons into the learners of the lesson box.

think about having a prize for those who have achieved

you might consider have 3 levels of prizes so all learners are rewarded

target Setting, Assessment, Feedback, pace and structure, digital technology

self, peer, employability, reflection and evaluation

Internet based resources

The internet is a great resource, I always encourage staff to research what's out there before reinventing the wheel, you might find exactly what you are looking for.

Wordle *(http://www.wordle.net/)* – *all levels*

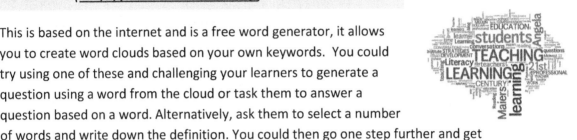

This is based on the internet and is a free word generator, it allows you to create word clouds based on your own keywords. You could try using one of these and challenging your learners to generate a question using a word from the cloud or task them to answer a question based on a word. Alternatively, ask them to select a number of words and write down the definition. You could then go one step further and get your learners to create online WIKIs based on the words, a good way to get your learners collaborating.

 If you want to jazz up a handout or resource, use your wordle as a washed out watermark. You could also ask your learners to generate their own wordle for the cover of their portfolio

 select a task from above for different learners based on their level

Q & A, Feedback, prior knowledge and understanding, Assessment, English, Stretch and Challenge, differentiation, structure, digital technology

prior knowledge and understanding, communication, English, linking theory to practice

Triptico Plus *(https://www.tripticoplus.com/) – all levels*

This website is a great teaching resource if you do not have access to an Interactive Whiteboard, all you need to do is create a free account and it gives you access to lots of dynamic customisable tools for teaching and learning, such as:

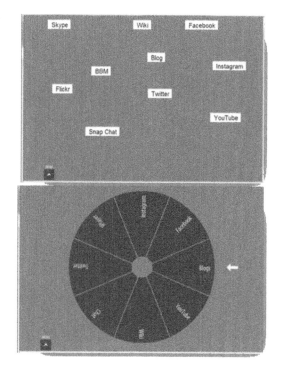

- **Word Magnets** are great to use for keywords, generate your keywords and get the learners to remove them as they have answered a question based on that keyword. Or simply just bounce differentiated questions around the room using them.

- **Text Spinner** this is good for generating questions populate the flipper with your own questions and watch it spin, once your question is selected you can use this to generate a good Q & A session going in your class.

It is really worth taking the time out to look at this website it's a great quick and easy tool to stimulate your learners using technology.

you can structure the activities around learner levels

you can sign up for a 30 day free trial. Once this has expired you will still be able to gain access to some of the activities but not all. However for a small fee you can purchase a licence

 Q & A, Assessment, Stretch and Challenge, Pace, structure, differentiation, Equality and Diversity, group work, digital technology

prior knowledge and understanding, self, peer, English, linking theory to practice, reflection and evaluation

Socrative *(http://www.socrative.com/) – all levels*

This is a student response system based on the internet again another wonderful free tool. You will need to create an account then download the teachers app to your PC or mobile device and get your learners to download the student app to their devices. Socrative allows you to create fantastic quizzes for quick learner feedback or fast assessment. Once created all you need to do is provide your learners with an access code which you will receive when you create your quiz, and you control the flow of questions from your app. It's a great way to introduce 'bring your own device' (BYOD).

If some learners don't have access to a smartphone put them into pairs or groups so they don't feel left out. You can also use this for learning outside the classroom.

Q & A, assessment, stretch and challenge, feedback, prior knowledge and understanding, pace, differentiation, digital technology

prior knowledge and understanding, self, peer, communication, linking theory to practice

Nearpod *(https://www.nearpod.com/) – all levels*

This is a way of downloading or creating interactive presentations. Once created you can share it with your learners in real time by controlling what and when they see content. Once they have access to the presentation they can submit comments or responses from a PC or mobile device and best of all you can track and record all responses making this an excellent way of recording and summarising engagement and assessment.

feedback, assessment, group work, stretch and challenge, independence, digital technology

self, peer, communication, reflection and evaluation

Google Drive *(https://www.google.com/drive/) – all levels*

A dynamic and easy to use tool promoting cooperative learning, learners can upload documents and peers can comment or edit them. It's an effective strategy to encourage students to work collaboratively with their peers. Google drive also works with all the Google apps so learners can create presentations online and incorporate multimedia into resources such as Youtube clips.

stretch and challenge, group work, assessment, feedback, structure, differentiation, equality and diversity, digital technology

self, peer, communication, employability, reflection and evaluation

Virtual Learning Environment (VLE)

It is standard practice now that most educational organisations have a VLE which is used as an assessment resource, a repository and a source for learning outside the classroom. Most organisation have their own name for this resource, for example Blackboard or Moodle. Elearning and VLE have been around a long time now and have gone through periods of success and disengagement. OFSTED are looking at it more closely now as they recognise the value to both the learner and the teacher. Over the years we have had a tendency to put all our classroom resources on our VLE and then proceed to still give them out in class. This effectively renders the VLE redundant. We need to change the culture of ELearning and how we use it, it should be about extending those learning opportunities outside the classroom giving them small snappy activities or dynamic ways of providing assessment evidence such as video or podcasts. These could then be introduced as an activity that they can do on the bus on the way home. That way they don't feel like it eats into their social time.

As a tool for assessment – *all levels*

The VLE can be used for online marking of assessments. By providing submission areas the learners can submit their work for marking and lecturers can view download review and comment and then re submit to the learner with a grade.

learners can work at their own pace at a time to suit them

stretch and challenge, group work, assessment, feedback, differentiation, equality and diversity, structure, digital technology

self, employability, communication, reflection and evaluation

VLE quizzes and games *– all levels*

You can set small activities that they can do as homework or even a more formal quiz. Keep them small and snappy, tell them they can do them on their mobile phones on the bus home. Make it easy for them.

 learners can do this in their own time without the stress of time frames and peer pressure

 stretch and challenge, group work, assessment, feedback, differentiation, prior knowledge and understanding, digital technology

self, peer, prior knowledge and understanding, reflection and evaluation

Powerpoint Quizzes – *all levels*

For those who don't have access to a smartboard, quizzes can easily be set up in PowerPoint using hyperlinking. You will need to create a number of pages:

- o   Main menu slide
- o   Question slides (no more than 10)
- o   Wrong Answer slide (you will need one for each question)
- o   Correct answer slide

Once you have created your questions it's better to stick to multi choice as its much easier to set up. You will need to start hyperlinking each answer to the *Correct* or *Wrong* slide. **NOTE**: you will need to put a hyperlink on the *Correct* or *Wrong* slides to take you back to where you want them to be, in the case of right answer slide you need to link back to the main menu page and in wrong answer back to the question slide so they can re try.

Your presentation should look like this:

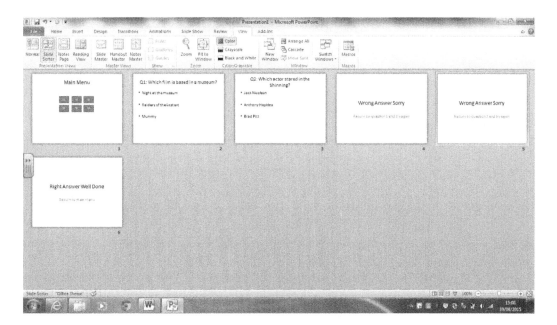

you need to decide how you are going to organise the game, using individual or group teams being careful to make the selection strategy fair and everyone engaging

 assessment, stretch and challenge, equality and diversity, English, maths, differentiation, digital technology

self, peer, prior knowledge and understanding, reflection and evaluation

Powerpoint for presentations – *all levels*

Powerpoint is the most popular software for presenting information, however, how many times have we watched one with lines and lines of text and the presenter reads each slide line by line, I don't know about you but there are times I have lost concentration or even found myself dropping off! I like to use Powerpoint very differently. I try not to use text where appropriate and instead use images to stimulate what interest I want to raise. The consequence of using this alternative strategy:

- o Prevents reading text line by line
- o Prevents filling the audience up with too much information
- o Creates an interesting visual
- o Generates interactive discussion when one is not dictated to by text

Take a risk, have a go and see what a difference it makes. Look at Pecha kucha, which means 20 slides 20 seconds each: http://www.**pechakucha**.org/.

using images instead of text supports the more visual learner

stretch and challenge, assessment, Q & A, feedback, differentiation, equality and diversity, prior knowledge and understanding, independence, digital technology

prior knowledge and understanding, self, reflection and evaluation

Prezi *(http://www.Prezi.com) – all levels*

This software is free on the internet. It allows you to create interactive presentations but goes that one step further than Powerpoint, as it has more dynamic animation. You can use the readymade templates or start from scratch or even convert one of your old Powerpoint presentations to a Prezi by simply uploading it.

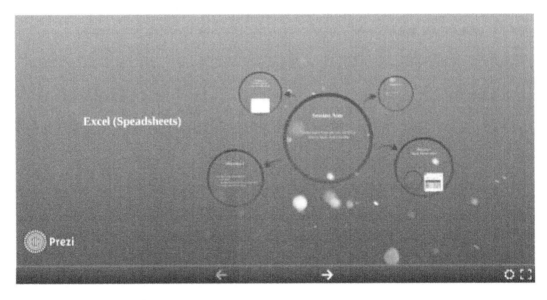

 *pace and structure, digital technology*

Google Classroom – *all levels*

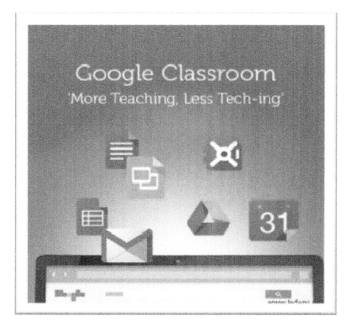

A reasonably new development from Google, this resource is becoming increasingly popular in Education and is potentially a good contender to the VLE. Google classroom is free to education providers, however, your IT department will have to register your site, then with a nominated admin person you can add teachers and students to your groups. You then have unlimited access to bring all the Google apps together under the classroom umbrella and allows you and your learners to make use of them collaboratively. These apps include:

- Drive for storing documents or uploading assignments for marking on line and providing secure feedback, these also facilitate collaboration and peer assessment.
- Calendars for sharing key information and dates
- Hangouts for providing a shared student community
- Gmail to communicate with each other
- Blogger for creating blogs
... and much more.

learners can engage in their own time at their own pace

 stretch and challenge, assessment, Q & A, feedback, structure, pace, differentiation, equality and diversity, group work, target setting, independence, digital technology

self, peer, employability, communication, reflection and evaluation

Digital dictionaries – *all levels*

Most smartphones now have access to a free downloadable app for dictionaries and thesaurus. These apps provide a positive way to use mobile phones in the classroom.

learners are encouraged to learn independently

English, independence, digital technology

English

Digital Glossaries – *all levels*

You can create these in VLEs whereby you and your learners can create new words and descriptions, try getting learners to add new words to the collaborative glossary at the end of each week.

learners are able to access this at anytime, anywhere to support their learning in and out of the classroom

assessment, English, Stretch and Challenge, differentiation

self, peer, English, communication

WIKI – *middle to high levels*

A wiki is a type of content management system that allows collaboration of content. A good alternative to a glossary, you could get learners to create words and descriptions and others can contribute with their own interpretations or ideas. This is a great resource which you can get learners to do weekly. The work they input could contribute to their formal assessments. A good example of WIKI's is Wikipedia: (*https://www.wikipedia.org/*).

learners are able to access this at anytime, anywhere to support their learning in and out of the classroom

stretch and challenge, assessment, feedback, structure, English, differentiation, equality and diversity, group work, target setting, independence, digital technology

self, peer, English, employability, communication, reflection and evaluation

Flipped Classroom – *middle to high levels*

The flipped classroom is becoming more and more popular now with the need to cover so much within the limits of the curriculum. More practical subjects lend themselves to this very well. The idea is that you video the skill or the taught segment of a lesson and the learners then access this remotely as many times as they like outside the classroom. For example within Beauty Therapy a facial massage routine could be recorded with a running commentary and then made available to your learners using your VLE or YouTube. You then instruct your learners to watch the video before the lesson. You can then plan a Q & A starter activity and reduce the time spent on demonstrating the routine in class time giving them more time to practice. This also provides revision material for when they practice at home.

WARNING

we know that learners are really good at not doing homework tasks set so do have a back up plan.

Helpful Tip!

As an example of a back up plan, send those who didn't watch the video somewhere to watch it, deliver your planned Q & A to those who did then ask them to devise questions to ask the others when they return.

learners are able to access this at anytime, anywhere to support their learning in and out of the classroom

stretch and challenge, assessment, Q & A, feedback, structure, pace, differentiation, equality and diversity, group work, target setting, English, prior knowledge and understanding, independence, digital technology

AFL

prior knowledge and understanding, self, peer, English, employability, communication, linking theory to practice, reflection and evaluation

There are some very good software resources you can use for the flipped classroom such as **TEDED, Educanon** and **EduPuzzle**. These allow you to create lessons in the software that your learners can access. The lesson can be created by anyone that creates an account, and it involves adding questions and discussion topics to any educational video or YouTube clip. The only slight difference is that EduPuzzle allows you to upload your own video. Once created you can give access to your learners by email and then you can monitor their assessment results through the software.

learners are able to access this at anytime, anywhere to support their learning in and out of the classroom

stretch and challenge, assessment, Q & A, feedback, structure, pace, differentiation, equality and diversity, group work, target setting, English, prior knowledge and understanding, independence, digital technology

prior knowledge and understanding, self, peer, English, employability, communication, linking theory to practice, reflection and evaluation

Flickr *(https://www.flickr.com/) – middle to high levels*

Flickr allows you to add images and albums. Privacy settings can be set so that only specific groups can see them add comments or tag each other on the images. Great for creating education trip photos or better still get learners involved in a project whereby they have to take photos when their out and about and upload them to Flickr. A great resource for the media and arts curriculums.

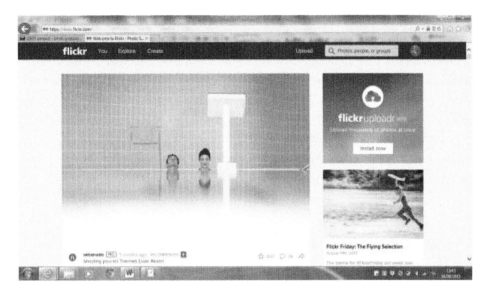

 learners are able to access this at anytime, anywhere to support their learning in and out of the classroom

 stretch and challenge, assessment, Q & A, feedback, structure, pace, differentiation, equality and diversity, group work, target setting, independence, digital technology

self, peer, employability, communication, reflection and evaluation

Youtube *(https://www.youtube.com) – all levels*

A globally popular video repository, you can create your own channel for you and your learners and upload videos such as skills tutorials, flipped classroom footage trips and visits and anything else that you create. You could even get your learners to create videos and get them to submit them to you for inspection before posting.

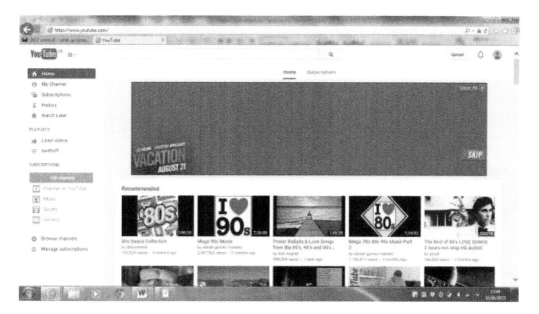

 learners are able to access this at anytime, anywhere to support their learning in and out of the classroom

 stretch and challenge, assessment, Q & A, feedback, structure, pace, differentiation, equality and diversity, group work, target setting, independence, digital technology

self, peer, employability, communication, reflection and evaluation

Podcasting – *all levels*

Podcasts are voice recordings that you can create simply on your smartphone or a Dictaphone. They are useful and effective for providing additional instructions for learners on homework tasks. You can even embed them into Powerpoint so it becomes a whole resource. Another way of using podcasting is to get your learners to record debates or even peer assessment. Learners sometimes find it difficult to put things into words but find it much easier to say what they mean rather than write. All mobile devices now allow you to record your voice and share it via email.

This is a good alternative for those who struggle with written literacy skills. Learners are able to access this at anytime, anywhere to support their learning in and out of the classroom.

stretch and challenge, assessment, Q & A, feedback, structure, pace, differentiation, equality and diversity, group work, target setting, independence, digital technology

self, peer, employability, communication, reflection and evaluation

Blogging *(https://www.blogger.com)* *– middle to high level*

Blogging is an effective way of encouraging learners to self reflect and evaluate on a particular subject or topic you have discussed. Blogs are made up of a series of text entries similar to a diary except you and their peers can comment and debate if the permissions are set up to do so. These have proved very popular within FE and HE as learners feel like they are creating their own website and they get a great sense of achievement from this when they start to express themselves. Good websites you can use are Blogger which is a Google product. It is easy to use and provides you with templates to get you going quickly

I set up a blog on our VLE which learners use to have programme specific conversations and ask each other questions. Do make sure though that you access it regularly to prompt conversation and debate and ensure its being used for the purpose it was set up for.

a safe environment for all learners to engage and encourage peer support but do make sure you check regularly for appropriate content

assessment, Group Work, differentiation, feedback, English, equality and diversity, independence, digital technology

self, peer, communication, reflection and evaluation

Pinterest *(https://www.pinterest.com/) – middle to high levels*

Pinterest is another fairly new development and its primary purpose is to create pinboards of things that you find of interest. When you sign up to Pinterest you specify what you are interested in so that it searches ideas and suggestions of things relating to your subject. If you find something you like you can pin it to your board, it's a bit like bookmarking in a visual way. You can create as many boards as you wish and then share them. Some good examples of using Pinterest for education is to search hair designs/styles for learners studying hairdressing; recipes for catering; art work for art and design or media. Think about tasking your learners to create pinboards for themselves and share them with their peers. Encourage them to comment on each other's boards and debate.

 learners can work both independently and with peer support to express themselves individually

assessment, Group Work, differentiation, feedback, English, equality and diversity, independence, digital technology

self, peer, communication, reflection and evaluation

Trello *(https://trello.com/) – middle to high levels*

This software is essentially a business administration application which lends itself nicely as a tool for planning assignments or work load for projects or course work. It allows you to create lists for example things to do, working on and completed. Example below:

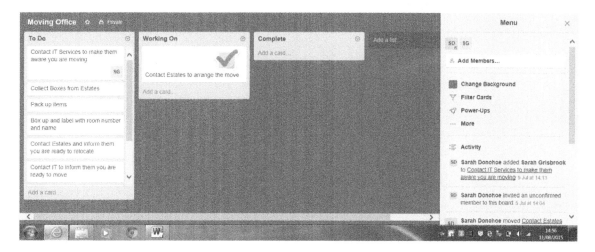

The above example shows the project name 'Moving Office' and 3 lists: 'to do', 'working on' and 'complete'. Under my lists I have tasks and as I complete a task I can simply drag it across to the appropriate list. A handy facility is that the software is collaborative so I can invite contributors to my project and then allocate a task to them. This software is perfect for groups working on projects as everyone can see their area of responsibility and where everyone else is up to. They can access this from their mobile devices and update as required. It's a very effective project management tool.

Learners can work both independently and with peer support. You can allocate group leader responsibilities for your stronger learners to stretch and challenge them.

stretch and challenge, assessment, Q & A, feedback, structure, pace, differentiation, equality and diversity, group work, target setting, English, independence, digital technology

self, peer, employability, communication, reflection and evaluation

QR Codes – *all levels*

These are the codes that you will have seen in shop windows or magazines that you can read by holding your mobile device up to it and it reads it using a scanning app, which then directs you to a website. You could embed these into your course handbooks making them more interactive or simply just putting them around the classroom you could then use them as extension activities for Maths or English, linking to interactive learning websites.

learners are supported as and when they need it

stretch and challenge, assessment, Q & A, feedback, structure, pace, differentiation, equality and diversity, independence, digital technology

communication, linking theory to practice

Augmented reality – *all levels*

This is similar to QR Codes but it directs you to a video that you have generated instead of a website. You could think about creating a video of something that you have to cover in your class on a regular basis such as a health and safety element and then learners can access at any time from a visual code in a handbook or on the classroom wall. You could even use it for rules and regulations.

learners are supported as and when they need it

stretch and challenge, assessment, Q & A, feedback, structure, pace, differentiation, equality and diversity, independence, digital technology

communication, linking theory to practice

NOTE: Using technology for learning is a great way to introduce yourself and your learners to more dynamic innovative ways to teach and learn and it's an exciting and enjoyable experience for both teachers and learners. Before engaging with any of these resources and activities, think about how and why you want to use it. Using technology is only valuable if it has an impact on learning so when planning to use digital technology, think about the impact before the need.

Just one final quote I would like to leave you with which I picked up from a recent technology conference:

"Technology won't replace teachers, but teachers who use technology will probably replace teachers who don't" (Wheeler 2013)

Chapter 9 – Reflection & Evaluation

Reflective practice is as important as the learning that precedes it. To be able to reflect on learning enables an individual to make sense of what they have learned and plan for future learning activities. It is believed to be one of the essential ingredients of the expert learner and I am sure you will agree that we would all love our learners to be expert at learning. This empowers learners in terms of taking ownership of their learning. However, although as educators, most of us are able to reflect effectively, don't presume that your learners know how to reflect. So you need to give them the tools to do this effectively to ensure the activity has the desired results.

There are plenty of models of reflection out there so you need to choose a model that best reflects the outcomes you are looking for your learners. I would suggest that you produce a proforma with questions on that prompt reflective practice; see '**Checking out**' in the Plenary chapter, or look at the other plenary activities, you'll see that they are all based on the foundations of reflective practice.

Learning Journal – *all levels*

Keeping a learning journal is a great way to structure and formalise reflections and it can also act as a motivator for learning and a record of their progress. You could structure it so that you ask about how they initially feel about a topic then have entries midway through then at the end. What the learner should see is how much they have learnt and how much more confident they are with a specific skill or knowledge. These are also very useful for learners to take on work placements and educational visits.

 this gives individuals the confidence to be honest without having to share and will help raise the confidence and motivation of all learners

Build this into your scheme of work so that you allocate time to complete these in class. Don't count on learners completing these in their own time. If reflective practice is part of the specification criteria, it becomes an alternative method of assessment instead of tagging it on to the end of an assignment.

assessment, Q & A, feedback, structure, differentiation, equality and diversity, target setting, prior knowledge and understanding, independence

prior knowledge and understanding, self, linking theory to practice, reflection and evaluation

Emotional Intelligence (EI) – *all levels*

You can use reflective practice to formalise self assessment of the hidden curriculum. The hidden curriculum are the skills learned in situ that are vital to help learners, especially the younger learners to develop their individual, social and employability skills. Most of the skills one needs to be successful in life and work are listed and categorised within the Emotional Intelligence philosophy. In 1990, Daniel Goleman, took the initial concept of emotional intelligence and combined it with other scientific theories on what constitutes this success in life and work and developed his own taxonomy. There are lots of good books out there and I've included Goleman's 1996 initial publication in the reading list to get you started. Goleman categorised EI as follows:

Self-awareness	**Social awareness**
Emotional self-awareness	Empathy
	Organisational awareness
Accurate self-assessment	Service orientation
Self-confidence	
Self-management	**Relationship Management**
Emotional self-control	Developing others
Transparency	Inspirational leadership
Adaptability	Change catalyst
Achievement orientation	Influence
Initiative	Conflict management
Optimism	Teamwork and collaboration

Themed EI – *all levels*

One way to use EI as a reflective activity is to theme a workshop for learners to self assess against. For example, if learners are doing a group work exercise or research task, you could ask them to reflect on their skills of team work, initiative and organisation skills. This could then culminate in a discussion on why these skills are important in life and work which will help them to reflect on how they can develop these skills further and use them to achieve and succeed.

 as this is an individual and personal activity, all learners have the opportunity to engage in a safe approach

 You could use the same proforma in subsequent sessions to record progress of the skills. You could also include peer assessment as some learners can be quite harsh on themselves or can't recognise their own strengths.

stretch and challenge, assessment, Q & A, feedback, structure, differentiation, equality and diversity, group work, target setting, prior knowledge and understanding, independence,

self, peer, employability, communication, linking theory to practice, reflection and evaluation

Reflective Log – *middle to high levels*

Reflection is usually required as a formally assessed element in the higher levels of learning. As a resource for the learners to build their reflective reports is a log that they add to throughout their programme. Reflection is a personal activity that people approach in their own way but it is useful to offer prompts to help the process. If finances allow, learners can be given a small log book where you can paste the following on the inside cover (*Adapted from Rolfe et al - 2001*):

What –	So what –	Now what –
is the situation?	does this teach me?	do I need to do to improve things?
am I trying to achieve?	was I thinking and feeling?	broader issues need to be considered if this action is to be successful?
actions did I take?	other knowledge can I bring to the situation?	
was the response of others?	is my new understanding of the situation?	
were the consequences – for myself/for others?		might I do differently in the future?
		might be the consequences of this action?

Learners need only to address those prompts that are appropriate for the context of the reflection. (***Excellence Gateway*** – online)

reflection as a personal independent activity allows all learners to record their private feelings and opinions and feel safe to do so

stretch and challenge, assessment, Q & A, feedback, structure, differentiation, equality and diversity, target setting, prior knowledge and understanding, independence

self, employability, communication, linking theory to practice, reflection and evaluation

Shoebox Activity – *middle to high levels*

This is an activity that I now use within the ITT programme after experiencing it myself under the guidance of its originator Dr Janet Hobley. Janet asserts this as a powerful tool for learning and has used this many times successfully in ITT and professional development programmes. As a general teaching activity, this can be used as an ice breaker and a handy tool for groups to share their experiences and skills at specific points within a programme, which in turn can help you in your planning.

The group are asked to collect around 6 artefacts that reflect their personality, experiences, strengths, skills. These should be placed in a shoebox or other container to be shared at the next session. There is no doubt that this helps to bond the group and each individual can see clearly those who they may have a natural alliance with.

Ensure there is a ground rule that no article could offend other members of the group This may take some time so do be prepared for it to take up over an hour of the session depending on the size of the group. Without fail, each time I have facilitated this, there are always some tears so be prepared to manage the activity sensitively.

learners have the opportunity for personal expression and often, it helps peers to appreciate and get to know each other

stretch and challenge, assessment, Q & A, feedback, structure, differentiation, equality and diversity, independence,

self, peer, communication, reflection and evaluation

Chapter 10 – The Hidden Curriculum

Just as it's vital that we cover the curriculum, we also have a responsibility to our learners to prepare them for work and life. We do this through the hidden curriculum, that is, all the stuff they need to develop their emotional, social and personal skills. We do this in a variety of ways – through group and individual tutorials, through creative activities and through providing extra curricula opportunities. When planning activities, you might want to consider using the Emotional Intelligence categories (see **Reflection and Evaluation**) to help you make the most of the strategy by adding other skills and learning opportunities.

There are some skills that although are required to be promoted under the Common Inspection Framework, are not outcomes in the curriculums we teach and therefore we must consider these vital but hidden skills. Examples include promoting equality and diversity, functional skill acquisition and independence in terms of empowering learners through high expectations, stretch and challenge.

Embedding Maths

Do take a look at the **Starter Activities** pages as there are some great fun maths activities. In my area of teacher training, only one or two units include any reference to mathematical calculations so I try to embed maths in a variety of fun ways. I'm lucky in that as I do a lot of lesson observations, I get to see some great ideas that I can then adapt for my own learners. Here is one courtesy of Cameron Steward:

Calculate Your Partner – *all levels*

 This serves two purposes as it's also a strategy to organise learners into pairs and/or groups.

Create a series of questions and answers on separate post it notes and try to cover a range of calculations – multiply, divide, percentage, fractions, addition. Stick these on the back of the chairs before learners arrive. Instruct learners that they have either a question or an answer on their notes. Learners then have to take their note and find their partner then sit with them. To ensure everyone has been challenged, instruct those with answers to check they are the right partner by repeating the calculation. I have taken this one further by also preparing the symbol of calculation on an A4 card and placing it on a table. All those who have calculated using that symbol then sit at that table. That way, you have also created random group tables. Just in case one or two learners don't attend, place the extra post its on the wall and instruct learners if they can't find their partner, it might be on the wall. See also *Jenga* in **Assessment for Learning**.

 this results in random group/pair selection so you may want to hand out the post its to individual learners

stretch and challenge, assessment, structure, maths, prior knowledge and understanding,

prior knowledge and understanding, maths

Maths teasers

There are many maths teasers and quizzes available on the web so have a look around. See also **Starter Activities**.

Maths Trivia – *all levels*

Add a bit of interest by including statistics into your sessions. For example,

In childcare ask learners to calculate:

If there are 305 children living in Newtown as looked after children, and the child population is 57,000, what is the percentage of looked after children?

In Art, ask learners to calculate:

In 2013, 6,031,574 people visited the National Gallery in London. Assuming the gallery is open 6 days a week, what is the average daily visitor rate?

In construction ask learners to calculate:

In total, 33,816 new homes were registered in the UK during 2014, compared to 31,739 for the corresponding period a year ago, what is the percentage increase?

Of course it means you have to do a bit of homework, but if you find an interesting fact, you could then extend the activity with a discussion and link it to learning on the programme

 this will help those less confident with maths to improve their skills through relevant activity

 stretch and challenge, assessment, Q & A, feedback, structure, pace, differentiation, equality and diversity, maths

maths, employability, communication, linking theory to practice, reflection and evaluation

Health and Safety Quiz – *all levels*

To spice up Health and Safety lessons and introduce statistics, create a table as example below and design a series of questions including some analytical ones to stretch and challenge such as: 4% of three day absences are caused by 'other' what would you consider 'other' to be? (Taylor 2013)

Cause of accident	Fatal accidents	Non–fatal major accidents	Over 3–day absence
People hurt by moving vehicles, flying objects, machinery; trapped by something collapsing or overturning	41%	25%	20%
People slipping, falling, tripping, handling, lifting, carrying, striking *against* something	3%	38%	61%
Falls from a height	44%	30%	11%
Harmful substance	—	2%	2%
Fire and explosion	2%	1%	1%
Electricity	5%	1%	1%
Other	5%	3%	4%

 you can create a series of questions with differing levels of complexity and target specific individuals

stretch and challenge, assessment, Q & A, feedback, structure, pace, differentiation, equality and diversity, group work, target setting, maths, prior knowledge and understanding

self, peer, English, maths, employability, communication, linking theory to practice

Embedding English

Just as it is important to check spelling and grammar when marking work, you can also include practicing English skills as part of learning. Here are a few examples.

Correct Me – *low to middle levels*

If learners need to do any extended reading, you can sabotage it by taking out all the punctuation and capital letters. As they read the extract, they need to correct all the errors.

you can create different versions with differing levels of complexity and target specific individuals

stretch and challenge, assessment, Q & A, differentiation, equality and diversity, target setting, English, prior knowledge and understanding, independence

prior knowledge and understanding, self, English, employability, communication reflection and evaluation

Comprehension – *all levels*

Following the reading of an extract, compose a list of questions to be answered.

You can vary the complexity of the questions to suit the level from simple where the answer is in the text to more complex such as asking for opinions or counter arguments. For higher levels, complex questions could be debated in small groups.

stretch and challenge, assessment, Q & A, feedback, structure, pace, differentiation, equality and diversity, group work, target setting, English, prior knowledge and understanding, independence

prior knowledge and understanding, self, peer, English, employability, communication, linking theory to practice, reflection and evaluation

Spell and define *– all levels*

I observed a version of this in a maths lesson, a great way to embed English within maths.

Prepare cards with technical words on them, then attach another card behind with a definition of that word. Put learners in pairs. The first one says the word to their partner who has to try to spell it (speaking not writing). The card is then passed to the speller who asks their partner to define it.

This can be adapted in various ways, for example, it could relate to tools or materials and instead of definitions, you could ask what they are used for or health and safety considerations.

 pair a strong and weak learner. You can give out cards to specific learners related to level

 make sure they don't cheat by peeking at the card they are answering

stretch and challenge, assessment, Q & A, feedback, structure, pace, differentiation, equality and diversity, group work, target setting, English, prior knowledge and understanding, independence

prior knowledge and understanding, self, peer, English, employability, communication, linking theory to practice, reflection and evaluation

Glossary of terms – *all levels*

Certainly, if learners will be learning new technical or academic language, it is to their advantage to create a glossary of terms. You should start this from day one so each time a new word is learned it is added. You just need a proforma of 2 columns, column one is for the term, column two for the definition. This will help with assignment writing and revision. It would also be a good idea for you to keep one too and upload it to your VLE.

you could ask the class to look up the definition on their phones to add an element of using digital technology.

every learner will have their own glossary to refer to and cn compose their definition in terms they understand

assessment, Q & A, structure, differentiation, equality and diversity, English, prior knowledge and understanding, independence, digital technology

prior knowledge and understanding, self, English, employability, communication, linking theory to practice

Embedding Equality and Diversity

You will need to do some homework here but it will be worth it to add that element of interest and widen knowledge of the subject. Here are a few suggestions to give you some food for thought.

Construction and the Built Environment:

❖ Discuss types of bricks/timber used for different environments e.g. earthquake/flood/dry or hot zones

❖ Different practices in different countries e.g. wattage, wiring, plumbing, H & S

Motor Vehicle:

❖ Different countries standards e.g. tyres; MOT; road tax; speed limits etc

❖ Countries of manufacture for models of cars then extend this to where that country is – display a big map

Business/AAT:

❖ Different practices e.g. Spanish banking practices; tax laws; wages; gender divide in industry

Sport:

❖ Doing group work? Put them in countries as teams – choose a different continent each time, task them to show you where the country is on a map. You could even ask them to make a picture of the national flag to put in the middle of their table or pin to their shirts.

Uniform services:

❖ Different uniforms from different countries – you could turn this into a quiz.

❖ Different practices/protocols/rules/regulations particularly use of weapons and power of arrest/restraint

Catering/Nutrition:

❖ Country of origin of different foods then get them to show you where the country is on a map. Themed sessions based on different countries traditional dishes.

Hair/beauty:

❖ These curriculum areas lend themselves nicely to embedding diversity by studying and practicing different hair and make up traditions and trends.

Add a 'did you know………………'. Do some homework and include a trivial but very interesting fact about something another country does, or historical practices. I call this the QI (quite interesting) moment.

you may want to take advantage of any learner within the group who is familiar with the topic which will enrich the session further

stretch and challenge, assessment, Q & A, feedback, structure, pace, differentiation, equality and diversity, prior knowledge and understanding,

prior knowledge and understanding, self, peer, employability, communication, linking theory to practice, reflection and evaluation

Languages

Take advantage of any learners in your class who can speak other languages. Learn new words or phrases each session to add something different. You could also replace a key word being used that session with its foreign equivalent to add some fun. This helps minority learners to integrate into the group and learners can show off their new language skills outside the classroom.

make sure you can trust the second language speaker to use appropriate translations!

for learners for whom English is not their first language, this will give them a chance to shine

stretch and challenge, differentiation, equality and diversity,

employability, communication,

Diversity is also about using your learners experiences, characteristics, traditions, religions and social and work settings to enhance the learning environment. Why tell them all about something that one or more of your learners could do just as well. Take advantage of the rich and interesting backgrounds of your learners – less homework for you.

Chapter 11 – The Wow Factor

I'm often asked what it is that makes the difference between a good lesson and an outstanding one. Often the difference is you. It's how you deliver the session and the techniques you use. Just having great activities and resources is not enough. When planning your activities you also need to think about how you are going to engage them, challenge them, and use techniques to constantly raise the bar. We are all guilty of 'telling' too much. When planning lessons, think about what they can do to learn something without you telling them. As discussed previously, good questioning techniques play a big part here. When attending a Bradley Lightbody event, we were tasked to teach our partner something just using questioning techniques. This is a great way to practice asking questions as it doesn't come naturally to everyone. I've now built this activity into my staff development and ITT sessions. Try it out with a friend or colleague, you'll be amazed at what you can do then transfer the technique to your sessions.

Geoff Petty has coined the term 'teaching without talking' . Its all about learning through doing rather than listening. I regularly feed back to trainee teachers following an observation that they worked too hard. It's a big temptation to show learners what you know, great for your credibility but not a lot of learning going on. Learners need to be able to construct their own meaning in order to learn and remember so give them the tools to do just that.

As an example, on the teacher training programme, we study the curriculum development module and study different models of curriculum design. It is quite complex and there was no way I was going to stand and deliver a Powerpoint presentation and expect them to understand. I split the group into 4 sub groups and gave them a model each to research. They were given a brief to ensure they researched and gathered the essential elements required. They then used the resource centre to conduct their research which I facilitated using Socratic questioning techniques. They then came back and created a poster which they could design themselves to explain the model simply and clearly. I then used the *Jigsaw* method (see page 68) to create new groups then used the *Trade Exhibition* method (see page 71) for them to present to their peers. We then had a whole group discussion using my prepared questions to critically analyse the pro's and cons, strengths and weaknesses and similarities of the models. I was satisfied that they had learnt a great deal that day, had a good understanding of the models and enjoyed the session. I didn't do anything at all really, I just made it happen with planned activities and resources. The only things I had to prepare were the questions for the plenary and the brief. Think about where you could use this strategy in your own teaching, particularly if you teach a lot of complex theories.

Steve Barcley, an Educational Consultant and author proposes,

> *'WOWs are events, creative lesson plans, games, changes in the environment or the rules, things out of the box or on the outer edge. They contain elements of novelty, spontaneity, quality, and fun. They surprise. They make people laugh and feel good inside. The point is to do something to elicit a WOW! from students, teachers, parents, and others. This can take the form of a big, broad, astonished and amazing WOW!! or a small, lower case, italicized wow, as when something is touching and meaningful. The purpose of a WOW is to grab attention'* (Barcley nd)

Enough said!

Picture the scene... *– all levels*

A technique that wowed me recently came from one of my student teachers. She asked the group to close their eyes while she used questioning techniques to get them to talk through a recap of the last lesson. There are a number of theoretical strategies that can be used here and one which started the light bulb going off in my head more than others was behaviour management.

When students have their eyes closed they naturally don't chat to each other or take a sneaky peak of their phone – how fabulous is that? It also makes them concentrate on your voice as the hearing sense is the only one being used.

This made me think of situations where this could be used. For example, when discussing health and safety you could talk them through the steps they need to take before they start a task. It could go something like this:

Imagine you have entered the workshop, what is the first thing you should do? Then what do you do? What do you need to check? What should it look like? What tools do you need to collect? And so on. You will soon find you have a calm and focussed group. Try it out.

less confident learners feel less visible during the Q & A

stretch and challenge, assessment, Q & A, feedback, structure, pace, differentiation, equality and diversity, prior knowledge and understanding, independence

prior knowledge and understanding, self, peer, employability, communication, linking theory to practice, reflection and evaluation

Postcards Home – *all levels*

Many years ago a colleague came up with a brilliant idea to try to address retention following long term breaks such as Easter and Christmas and between academic years on long courses. During induction week, the learners were asked to write on a postcard their reasons for studying the programme and their hopes for the future on completion. They then addressed it to themselves and returned them to the tutor. One week before they were due to return to study, they were posted out to them. Many of the returning students thanked the teacher for reminding them of their motives and goals and were glad to be back. So, if attendance or drive is waning, try this out.

learners have the opportunity to express themselves safely and use their own aspirations to motivate them

feedback, differentiation, equality and diversity, target setting, independence,

self, reflection and evaluation

Differentiation Station – *all levels*

It is always tricky to know what to do when learners or groups of learners finish activities before others. If you do nothing and just let them wait, they will of course start to chat and check their phones, worse of all, may become disruptive. A strategy to use is to prepare an area where learners can go and do another activity while they wait. We call this a *Differentiation Station* and I've also seen this called simply the *Extension Table*.

Prepare a range of short activities ranging from easy to complex. They can be on anything related to the curriculum and functional skills, so for instance, a worksheet or crossword or even some basic maths and English exercises. The example below is from beauty therapy and tasks learners to answer the labels on the equipment – this strategy can be used for any curriculum area on any equipment and materials or even used as part of the lesson.

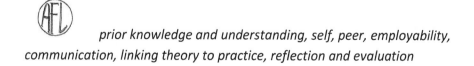

learners have the choice to experiment. Where appropriate, you can select the resource to try

stretch and challenge, assessment, Q & A, feedback, structure, pace, differentiation, equality and diversity, prior knowledge and understanding, independence

prior knowledge and understanding, self, peer, employability, communication, linking theory to practice, reflection and evaluation

And finally...

I do hope you enjoy using some of the activities and resources in this toolkit. I would be thrilled if you would let me know how it worked out for you and if you have adapted any of the activities. As I still work full time in the sector, I'm sure that it won't be long before an extended edition is in progress as I improve my own practice and observe brilliant teaching and learning.

You just need to take a risk now and then, if it doesn't work then adapt it or try something else.

Enjoy!

Reading List

Boyd Brewer. C (2008) Soundtracks for Learning: Using Music in the Classroom. LifeSounds Educational Services

Brewer C and. Campbell D.G. (1991) Rhythms of Learning: Creative Tools for Developing Lifelong Skills. Zephyr Press

Excellence Gateway www.excellencegateway.org.uk

Gilbert. I (2007) The Little Book of Thunks Carmarthen Wales. Crown House Publishing

Goleman. D (1996) Emotional Intelligence: Why it Can Matter More Than IQ Bloomsbury Publishing PLC

John Hopkins School of Education online at http://education.jhu.edu/PD/newhorizons/strategies/topics/Arts%20in%20Education/brewer.htm

Sky sports (online) https://livingforsport.skysports.com/mentors/six–keys–success

Taylor. G. (2013) Maths and English for Construction Cengage Learning

References

Barcley. S. online at http://barkleypd.com/blog/wow–adding–pizzazz–to–teaching–and–learning/

Bostock. J. and Wood. J. (2012) Teaching 14–19. A Handbook. Berkshire. Open University Press

Cowley. S. (2006) Getting the Buggers to Think . London. Continuum.

Excellence Gateway online http://repository.excellencegateway.org.uk/fedora/objects/import–pdf:1670/datastreams/PDF/content

Maths is Fun online at http://www.mathsisfun.com/index.htm accessed 12/1/14

Cooperative Learning online http://edtech.kennesaw.edu/intech/cooperativelearning.htm accessed 2/1/15

Rolfe G, Freshwater D & Jasper M (2001). *Critical Reflection for Nursing and the Helping Professions*.

Basingstoke, UK: Palgrave Macmillan

Smith. J. (2010) *The Lazy Teachers Handbook* Wales. Crown House Publishing Ltd

Gilbert. I (2007) *The Little Book of Thunks* Carmarthen Wales. Crown House Publishing

West–Burnham, J. & Coates, M. (2005) *Personalizing Learning* Stafford. Network Educational Press

Wheeler (2013). *Technology Won't Replace Teachers, But...* Retrieved from Learning with 'e's: My thoughts about learning technology and all things digital web site: http://steve–wheeler.blogspot.ca/2013/03/technology–wont–replace–teachers–but.html#!/2013/03/technology–wont–replace–teachers–but.html

Lightning Source UK Ltd.
Milton Keynes UK
UKOW05f2317181215

265023UK00004B/98/P